Country Color

Judith Miller
Country Color

PERFECT PALETTES FOR EVERY ROOM

Photography by Simon Upton

THE VENDOME PRESS

New York

To John, Tom, and Fred the Airedale

First published in the United States of America in 2009 by
The Vendome Press
1334 York Avenue
New York, NY 10021
www.vendomepress.com

Library of Congress Cataloging-in-Publication Data
Miller, Judith, 1951-
  Country color : perfect palettes for every room / by Judith Miller ;
photography by Simon Upton.
     p. cm.
  Includes index.
  ISBN 978-0-86565-254-5
  1. Color in interior decoration. 2. Decoration and ornament, Rustic. I.
Upton, Simon, 1967- II. Title.
  NK2115.5.C6M54 2009
  747'.94—dc22
                          2009007405

Publisher of U.K. Edition: Jacqui Small
Editorial Manager: Lesley Felce
Designer: Maggie Town
Editor: Sian Parkhouse
Editor of the U.S. Edition: Sarah Davis
Contributing Writer: Jill Bace
Location Researcher: Nadine Bazar
Production: Peter Colley

Distributed in North America by Harry N. Abrams, Inc.

Printed in Singapore
First printing 2009

Paint and Fabric Swatches
The paint and fabric palettes are the
author's own suggestions for successful
color combinations, and are not
intended to replicate the exact colors
and materials used in the rooms shown.

contents

what is country color?

The power of color to transform surroundings, to evoke a broad assortment of reactions, to touch the imagination, to exhilarate, excite, and inspire is unmatched. From the dawn of civilization, color has played a key role in the expression of man's creativity, the stimulation of the senses, and his enthusiasm for life.

introduction

Above Nestled into the lower slopes of the Sangre de Cristo Mountains near Santa Fe, New Mexico, the adobe structure and the massive local boulder steps mirror the colors of the desert environment.

Opposite The tapestry of colors formed by the lavender bushes, box hedges, and lemon and olive trees create the perfect backdrop for this Tuscan farmhouse.

Previous pages Tuscan rooms are not always painted in glorious terra-cotta: pale colorwash shades of off-white and pale green are cool escapes from the heat of the Italian summer in this farmhouse designed by Piero Castellini Baldissera.

COLOR ORIGINATES WITH NATURE. From the green of the landscape, the blue of the sky and sea, the yellow of the golden sun, and the eye-catching accent of the crimson found in a display of feathers, a coxcomb, or bright berries—nature not only is the source of ideas for colors, but also provides the colors themselves in the form of natural dyes and pigments. The oldest colors come from the earth, such as ocher and umber from clay, while colors obtained from animals and vegetables include madder, indigo, and cochineal from crushed beetles.

The heart of country style lies with nature and the land. Across the globe, from New England to Tuscany, North Africa to the Netherlands, and California to Bordeaux, country lifestyle is interpreted in a variety of ways. It is the colors of the landscape, the quality of the light, the climate, and the natural materials at hand for building and decorating that give voice to the colors of country style. The faded pink, reddish-brown terra-cotta, yellow ocher, and burnt sienna found in the rolling hills of the Tuscan landscape are reflected in the colorful decoration of a stone villa nestled

Above, left The warm pink of the local stone of this 1870 farmhouse in Tarn et Garonne in southwest France is offset by the pale blue of the wooden shutters and the rich fabrics on the 19th-century painted-metal daybed. The shutters were originally painted with woad, which is a natural insect repellent.

Above, center Local stone and pale gray shutters with climbing roses and olive trees create the idyllic setting for this 19th-century Tuscan farmhouse, near the hilltop village of Montalcino.

Above, right The natural colors of the adobe structure mirror the colors of the high desert in Santa Fe, New Mexico.

in the countryside. A humble dwelling in southern Spain pays homage to an exotic tradition that looks for inspiration to North Africa and the Moors for a rich vocabulary of vibrant yellows, blues, pinks, and greens tempered by cool whites, warm golds, and sands. In Sweden and in North America the decoration of a traditional farmhouse or cottage tends to boast the bracing, chilly colors—pale blue, gray, crisp white, and pale yellow—evocative of northern climates. Like seasonal change, travel can open the eye to new perceptions of color under different light.

Cultural sources such as these enhance the excitement of intense color. When juxtaposed side by side, nature's vibrant, saturated shades or pale, muted hues create crisp contrasts that will brighten and enliven, both inside and out, a house that celebrates country style. Contrasts of color may also be used to highlight architectural details, for instance the deep blues used to pick out frames and architraves on whitewashed Greek island houses. Shutters, doors, verandas, balconies, and window frames might be artfully arranged and painted to clash brightly with the walls in a joyous use of color. In parts of the world with limited resources and luxuries rare and few, the application of rich colors serves not only to decorate, but to gratify the senses and spirit as well.

In many cultures the use of color has traditionally designated one's status in society. The interiors of wealthy Colonial households, for example, were frequently decorated in sumptuous pigments that were usually imported and therefore extremely

expensive. Rich gilding enhanced colors such as Prussian blue—derived from the costly mineral lapis lazuli—vermilion, and verdigris, which were employed to produce a range of strong, saturated blue and green tones. In less prosperous homes and in rural areas where imported pigments were rarely available, a range of warm and subdued hues—yellow ochers, cane yellows, pinkish reds, and sage greens—tended to originate from the colors of local clays, soils, plants, and even animal blood.

Colors in all their diversity and in imaginative and rich combinations give life to humble country interiors. The eye is at home with hues that work in harmony together—pale and dark shades of the same tint or robust and lively color combinations that marry complementary but "opposite" colors such as red and green.

Proportion is the key to achieving successful color combinations. Where a dash of contrasting color can be refreshing, too many colors competing for attention will feel awkward and uncomfortable. Although prevailing decorating wisdom holds that light colors open up small dark rooms, in fact it is warm shades—reds, yellows, and oranges—that are welcoming and intimate, giving small rooms and closed-in areas an inviting jewel-like brilliance that compensates for the lack of space. Pale neutral colors and pastels underscore the spacious and airy atmosphere found in rooms that benefit from a great amount of natural light. In the end, the origins of a color scheme to decorate a country interior might ultimately be found in something close to home: a favorite painting, a treasured ceramic bowl, or a much-loved tapestry or carpet.

Above, left The spectacular Fall colors in Upstate New York have been an inspiration for interior colors for centuries.

Above, center A wooden cabin blends seamlessly onto this tiny island in the Oslo fjord. The natural colors are provided by the stones, trees, sea, and sky.

Above, right The blended colors of the fields and trees in southern France provide the backdrop for a Provençal palette.

This page The pale pink on the exterior walls of this farmhouse, built in 1915 in the south of Holland, picks up the tones from the brick patio.

Opposite In rural Normandy, the courtyard of an old coaching inn, built in 1830, has a wonderful country garden feel. The flowers and herbs are controlled by box hedges. The original timber-frame structure is softened by an overall limewash, whose muted tones pick up the flower colors.

Country style is irrevocably linked with the landscape from which it emerged; its colors and tones are very much a product of the bounty of the countryside. Materials such as wood, stone, and earth form the structure of a country home, and their natural beauty establishes a variety of palettes.

natural materials

wood Over the years timber adopts a mellow, timeworn gloss both outside and in. The window shutters of a cottage in Upstate New York fade and weather, pitched roofs on a Swiss chalet acquire a green patina that is bleached by the sun, while an ocean-side clapboard farmhouse on the coast of Maine takes on silver gray shadows that are the result of frequent exposure to the seasonal whims of sunshine and rain, wind and snow. Inside, the inherent colors of woods used for wall paneling, door frames, or floor planks continue to deepen and eventually realize a mellow glow. These subtle changes mark the passage of time, an effect which remains a key component of country style.

A cherished natural resource found in the surrounding landscape, wood has for centuries been a readily available material for building houses, constructing furniture, and decorating interiors in the country style. The lodges

Above Perched on a hill above the Rappahannock River in Virginia, this wooden cabin has a traditional beamed construction chinked with naturally pigmented Portland cement.

Left The design of the traditional Douglas fir ceiling in the great room of this home in Santa Fe, New Mexico, by Archaeo Architects, was influenced by Japanese design. The light from the high windows brings visual focus to the wooden structure.

Opposite In this Tuscan farmhouse the wood-beamed ceiling is left exposed. The terra-cotta flooring and local-stone-and-brick arch ground the building. The furniture, designed by Anthony Collett for this house, shows influence of the Arts & Crafts movement.

I take up my pen in the year of grace 17——, and go back to the ... 'ral Benbow' inn, and the brown old seaman, with th...

and cabins built by pioneering New Englanders and Pennsylvania Dutch settlers in timber-rich America enjoy much in common with the traditional farmhouses sprinkled across Scandinavia and the quaint thatch-roofed cottages nestled in the English countryside. All share a dependence upon native woods to create the structural elements of a country dwelling—pitched or gabled roofs, ceiling beams, high vaulted ceilings, and floorboards which promise to become decorative features in their own right—as well as additional embellishments that include free-standing and built-in furniture, window frames, blinds and shutters, wall paneling, and elaborately carved and turned banisters and staircases.

Although it can be defenseless against the damage brought about by wood-boring insects, this solid, robust, and flexible material derived from the trunks of trees boasts unique qualities of stability, durability, color, texture, elasticity, and hardness—all of these properties give it pride of place as the ideal material for building and furnishing a house in the country style.

A variety of woods indigenous to countries across the globe can be divided into two principal groups—hardwoods that originate from broad-leaved trees such as beech, oak, ash, elm, and chestnut and the softwoods produced by conifers including pine, spruce, cedar, and

Left From the exposed beamed ceiling structure to the wooden floor in this workman's cottage in Upstate New York, the color palette is dominated by deep pine tones, contrasted with the coolness of the white walls.

Opposite The natural oak beamed and columned structure and plank door brings the overwhelming warmth of wood to this nautically inspired kitchen, designed by Johnny Grey.

Above This New Zealand house, by Architectus, built in an Auckland suburb, is constructed from a light wooden frame. Wood is used as cladding and wall-cover, for the ceilings and the floor boards. The natural honey and golden tones are preeminent in the color scheme.

17

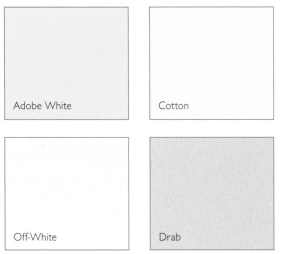

Adobe White

Cotton

Off-White

Drab

COLOR PALETTE With strong wood tones, natural pigments can work best. Off-whites and cool creams allow the intrinsic warmth of the wood to predominate.

Right and Below In the hallway of a Santa Fe adobe house, the entrance to the great room (the main living area) is dominated by a traditionally designed Douglas fir arch. In the hallway leading off this room wooden screens have been used to draw the eye to the guest wing. The design, by Archaeo Architects, is traditional in New Mexican homes.

Opposite The rustic chestnut-beam structure is exposed in this Perigord *chartreuse*. Beams such as these would originally have been plastered over, if the room was used for guests, but the current owner felt the natural wood from the region was too beautiful to be hidden.

yew. Each species of timber plays a special role in the composition and decor of a rural dwelling. While the construction of houses has traditionally relied upon the strength and durability of oak, for example, the color, close grain, and hardness of woods such as walnut and mahogany make them ideal for making furniture. The quality of light also plays a key role in the perception of the color of the chosen timber. The rich warm color of a table or chair made from the hardwood mahogany that furnishes an interior in the relentless bright white glare of the sundrenched towns in the Caribbean or South America, for example, assumes a decidedly different glow in the cool gray light of a snug cottage in the northern climates of England, Ireland, and the Netherlands.

Alongside the craftsmanship that defines the rural past and the country way of life lie the strength and durability of wood. It is one of the most beautiful and organic of all materials to be found in the world's vast landscape. In its natural state, wood reveals a host of multi-patterned grains and depths of colors. Key structural elements—such as the ceiling beams found in a house in New Mexico and those that inform a modest *ryokan* in Japan—share the beauty of wood unadorned and are decorative features in their own right. Yet the type of wood used and the quality of light—in the daytime, at dusk, by candlelight or firelight—will affect the perception of the

timber's true color and produce a medley of magical effects that alter from day to day, season to season. Subtle, continuously changing hues of color, light, and shade conspire to create a dazzling display of visual effects in rooms where walls, floors, doors, window frames, chairs, tables, and cabinets are made of wood.

But wood can also lend itself to a variety of time-honored techniques for furniture and interior decoration, including painting, carving, and graining, veneering, gilding, and lacquering. By its very nature a country dwelling looks to simple and uncomplicated decorative schemes. When natural wood is treated with wax polish, wood stain, or varnish, the beauty of the grain is enhanced. Deep earth colors made from natural mineral pigments—terra-cotta, blue, brick red, and moss green—were frequently favoured for the wall paneling and furniture found in the American Colonial interior, while the country style of Gustavian Scandinavia looked to the bracing, chilly tones mirrored in the surrounding terrain, including shades of icy white and cream, pale pink, soft gray, and sky blue.

The ground-level floors of houses were traditionally made of beaten earth, flagstones, or slate paving, but wood came into its own as the material of choice for floors when houses grew to more than one story. A stylish feature in any country-style dwelling, floorboards—from early times sawn by hand resulting in varying thicknesses and widths—have been made from a variety of timbers whose natural beauty enhances an interior. The color and beauty of the grain become decorative features, especially if the planks are simply coated with oils for protection. For its hardness and durability, its pale color, and its handsome figure, elm has proven to be more desirable than oak.

The practise of applying paint to furniture and architectural woodwork was useful not only for bringing color and light into what might have been a rather dreary interior, but also helped to camouflage timbers of inferior quality and to conceal any flaws in the grain of the wood. With the passage of time, painted wood acquires an appealing patina that evokes the rural past.

Opposite In this paneled room, in a house designed by John Saladino, the paint has been distressed to show the layers of historic paintwork. The overall impression is gray white with a rough texture. The oak ceiling beams have been limed.

Right, above In this ski chalet in Taos, New Mexico, a traditional feel is created by faux chinked beams, Native American prints, and warm-toned fabrics.

Right, center This early 20th-century Norwegian cabin has stained pine beamed walls. They form a stark contrast to the traditional white-painted-plaster corner fireplace and the fresh blue-and-white fabrics.

Right, below Stained pine boards on floors and walls dominate the comfortable relaxing area in this home in the mountains in Norway. The dark brown tones are picked up in the throw and cushions on the daybed.

stone

For thousands of years stone has been the linchpin for the building and decoration of houses. A natural building material, stone in an array of guises can be found in all parts of the world. Stone conveys a warm, informal, and rustic atmosphere to a country-style interior, and it is well-matched with other materials for architectural features such as roof tiles made of terra-cotta or ceiling beams, door frames, and floor boards constructed from local timbers including chestnut, walnut, or oak.

The enduring appeal and timeless integrity of stone make it an ideal building material for architecture in the country-house style. In every incarnation, in every shade—from limestone to marble, from granite to sandstone—the modest and rustic character of the country house made of stone is celebrated. A house built wholly or partly of stone reflects the soft, timeworn colors of the surrounding landscape; inside walls, floors,

and fireplace surrounds constructed from stone carry the color, warmth, and texture of the countryside into a cozy kitchen or tranquil bedroom, while a variety of bold, rough-hewn shapes and sizes of stone create patterns that play a decorative role. The pale and muted color palette of stone, boasting shades of taupe, platinum, charcoal, or slate gray, evokes the simple, uncluttered tranquility of the countryside.

Around the globe the color of stone is influenced by the quality of light as well as tradition. The thick walls of

Left The stone for this 18th-century farmhouse is local to the Orcia valley in Tuscany. Originally this was a two-up, two-down house; the family would have lived above, with the animals safely housed in quarters below.

Left The internal corridor of this adobe house in the desert close to Santa Fe is dominated by the massive stone wall chosen from a quarry in Telluride, Colorado by the architect and owner. They chose the stone for its various tones of gray. This is also reflected in the banded limestone floor. The lighter gray is from Portugal, the darker from Spain.

Opposite The scale of this wooden-beamed cabin in the north-east of Norway is more Adirondack camp than small "cabin in the woods." The design, by Helene Forbes-Hennie, is more modern than traditional, with sharper lines. The comfortable sofas pick up tones from the local stone.

a weathered stone farmhouse, or *mas*, reflect the intense, glowing colors of the rural Provençal landscape, while a low-built villa in Tuscany relies on the time-honored practise of covering stone walls with stucco in shades of pale pink or golden ocher. Flagstones pave the floor of an English cottage kitchen, the courtyard of a Spanish hacienda wears a stone chip pattern, and in Virginia a cabin in the hills gains warmth from a rough-hewn fireplace.

From country to country the color, composition of minerals, strength, and hard-wearing properties of the indigenous stone tend to determine how and where it is used—for the sumptuously carved detail on a decorative column, the rough-hewn fire surround of a rural country cottage, or the unevenly laid tiles on a sun-drenched terrace. Neighborhood quarries traditionally supplied the stone needed for the construction of country dwellings—from the rich marble deposits of Carrara in Italy to the strip mines of Colorado—with exceptions made to accommodate demand for a particular color or quality of stone that was unavailable locally.

Across the globe country architecture has relied on a number of different types of stone over the centuries, among them limestone, marble, and sandstone. Easy to shape, soft sedimentary limestone is composed of calcium

carbonate and found in a wide range of colors and textures; it welcomes delicate detail and has been used since antiquity for building, architectural carving, and sculpture. Time and again the soothing, understated ambience of the country-house interior has been well-served by the use of limestone—for example, a carved fireplace surround, a sturdy kitchen sink, or floor tiles made of flagstone. Boasting a rainbow of colors ranging from creamy gray to yellow, brown, or red, travertine—a hard limestone that was used extensively for building by the ancient Romans—continues to hold sway as a popular modern cladding material.

Synonymous with the architecture of Italy, marble enjoys a distinguished position as the building fabric of choice. It can be regarded as grand, because of the expense of transporting such a heavy material, but it should be remembered that it is an important component in relatively humble homes that are close to any area where marble is quarried: the key to country style is, of course, to employ local materials. Comprised mainly of calcium carbonate, marble is nothing more than limestone that has been altered by heat or pressure. White marble is created from calcium carbonate in its purest form. Other ingredients found in limestone—such as iron or clay—will also be transformed, resulting in highly

Left In Mimmi O'Connell's converted schoolhouse in the south of Tuscany, the main color aspect comes from the original inexpensive terrazzo floors. The contrast between the combination of terra-cotta, yellow, gray, beige, and chalky white of the floor and the monastic simplicity of the walls and ceiling leads the eye to the hint of the exotic—an ornate painted door from Lombok.

Opposite The muted tones of ancient stone used for the floor set the scene in this house in the Dordogne region of France. The subtle shading is the perfect backdrop for off-white painted 19th-century chairs.

Below In this adobe house near Santa Fe, designed by Baker-Laporte and Associates, the main fire-stack is built with local stone in the traditional manner. The warm tones of this stone are mirrored in the Arizona stone floor.

Right The fieldstone in this internal wall has a wide variety of tones, which are echoed in the furnishings. Even the color of the mortar is reflected in the painted cupboard. The beams, cabinet top, and window frame are painted in obsidian— a brown-based gray.

Below, left The walls of exposed Connecticut fieldstone in this Federal house built in 1827 served as inspiration for interior designer Jeffrey Bilhuber's color choices. The taupes, platinum, and grays complement the natural hues of the stone.

Opposite In the main bedroom of this house, built around 1800 in Northern Pennsylvania, the focal point is the local stone. The early English and German settlers used building techniques brought from Europe. The coursed random rubble walls made of rough-faced stones are laid with great attention paid to color, shape, and texture.

prized marbles in a range of sumptuous colors. From ancient times marble—which can be found across the world—has been chosen for building, architectural ornament, and sculpture. While limestone tends to convey a more informal character, marble can bring an opulent tone to the country house interior when favored for the glossy sweep of a tiled floor, for lining the walls of a bathroom, or as the sumptuously carved fireplace forming the striking focal point of a sitting room.

Sandstone has long been a favored material for the construction of country-house architecture as well as for decorative embellishments, including paving and carving. At home in most corners of the world, this sedimentary building stone remains especially familiar in southern Italy, the island of Sicily, southern Spain, and the north of England. Formulated from grains of quartz mixed with sand, it can be found in a wide variety of vibrant hues, ranging from bright white, yellow, red, and blue to brown and shades of pale gray. Yorkstone—the particular variety of faded, fine-grained sandstone originating in south Yorkshire in England—continues to make its mark not only as a building stone but, as it is equally durable both inside and outdoors, for roof tiles and for paving country-style kitchen floors and rustic garden terraces. The color of all varieties of stone brings warmth and softness to a house dedicated to country style.

COLOR PALETTE Fieldstone is a seemingly endless source of color inspiration, with all tones of gray, off-white, and taupes.

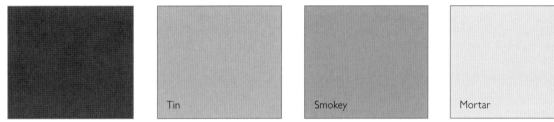

Cannon

Tin

Smokey

Mortar

earth For thousands of years the soil has brought forth a host of materials essential for building, including wood, stone, and the soft sedimentary rock known as clay. Key to the building of a country dwelling since antiquity has been the humble brick, made by pressing into a mold a type of clay known as brickearth, which then hardens by the processes of sun-drying or firing. The type of brickearth and additives used, along with the firing temperatures and methods for shaping, determine not only the texture, but the durability and color of the bricks as well. Historically, rural architecture has looked to the surrounding countryside for inspiration, yielding an array of robust farmhouses, rustic barns and lodges, and cozy cottages that seem to spring from the earth.

For generations brick has been a dependable bulwark for the architecture of the country house. Sun-dried brick, or adobe, is not only a strong and reliable material for the exterior construction of a dwelling, but its reddish-brown hue brings color and warmth to an interior. There is a place in both a humble cottage

Opposite, far left New Mexico is the only state in the U.S. that has an unbroken tradition of adobe (sun-baked brick) building. The colors for the external walls are governed by law, to make sure buildings do not detract from the natural surroundings of the high desert. The walls reflect the color of the native Russian sage and Apache plume.

Opposite, left The *adoberos* (who lay the adobes) are highly skilled. These earth-plastered walls are hand troweled to form perfect arches. The floor is covered in Arizona buff stone and the fire-stack is built from local stone. With all the materials locally sourced by designer Paula Baker-Laporte, the colors blend seamlessly.

Opposite, below In the master bedroom the walls are again adobe, with a pigment added to the plaster for color. The shape of the ceiling was taken from old Santa Fe homes. The earth cover between the *vigas* (beams) was originally flat and had a tendancy to leak. It was re-plastered to stop the leaks and over time took on this coved shape.

Right The floor in both this room and the master bedroom on the left has a gravel base covered with earth. Traditionally they would be sealed with ox blood, but in these vegan homes they are finished with natural oils.

Pink Rose

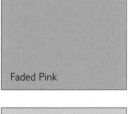

Faded Pink

Sand

Desert Dust

COLOR PALETTE Earth tones vary widely depending on geographic location. As bricks were traditionally made on site, colors came from the local landscape.

Left In this converted 15th-century Italian monastery designed by Paulo Badesco the traditional local pale red brick of the vaulted ceiling adds warmth to this kitchen. The modern inclusion of floor-to-ceiling glass panels brings the outside in. In the 15th century, the monks would have ensured these storage areas for wine were kept dark and cool.

of Spain where a country dwelling boasts the rich color of burnt sienna walls, floors paved with terra-cotta or quarry tiles, a host of terra-cotta pots lining a veranda, and the sun-baked red roof tiles that offer protection from the blistering rays of the sun.

Other materials which owe their origins to the clay of the earth and have proven extremely practical and effective for the exterior as well as the interior construction of a country dwelling are cement and plaster or stucco. A fine gray powder obtained by heating limestone and clay, cement dates from Roman times and in its modern incarnation is a hard, gray, and impervious fabric that, when mixed with sand, can be used both as a

Left The main color tones in this Belgian kitchen come from the muted multi-colored local terra-cotta tiles on the floor. Almost any color choice could be dictated by picking out any of the contrasting tones within the tiles.

Below The pale green clouded colorwash on the walls and off-white painted furniture in this Tuscan farmhouse kitchen are off-set by the original terra-cotta tiles. The colors of terra-cotta are as varied as the colors of the earth itself, from sand to dark red.

nestled in the Yorkshire Dales and a whitewashed Mediterranean palazzo in southern Italy for a timeworn kitchen floor, a rustic chimneypiece, or a sun-baked patio made of brick. Practical as well as hard-wearing, brickwork surfaces add a homespun, rustic atmosphere to the simple structure of a room and are happily matched with architectural features made from stone (such as floors or fireplaces) and wood (ceiling beams, doors, or staircase banisters) thereby creating a relaxing, lived-in setting for robust tables, chairs, and cabinets in the country style.

Terra-cotta is another material originating from the earth that is closely connected to the production of brick. Formed by molding or modeling clay and firing it to create a hard and durable body, terra-cotta can then be richly embellished with colorful paints or glazes to become a decorative feature of an architectural structure. While the materials and techniques employed to make both terra-cotta and brick are strikingly similar, the composition of terra-cotta clay typically tends to be more fine-grained and pliable, which allows for a depth of modeling and delicately carved detail.

Terra-cotta, the local clay of Tuscany—meaning "baked earth" in Italian—plays a key role in the decoration of country houses nestled in the countryside of hot and sunny climates including southern Italy, Spain, Portugal, and Provence. The ripe, reddish-brown color stretches widely across the sizzling landscapes of the Mediterranean, such as the scorching southern coast

Right Terra-cotta tiles, produced locally and so reflecting the color of the earth in that area, provide the warm accent to this quintessentially English country cottage kitchen.

Opposite In the original kitchen of this country house in the Dordogne region of France, local terra-cotta tiles on the floor were a pleasing and practical choice. The gray blue of the woodwork and warmth of the floor are complemented by the fresh yellow walls.

Below The bricks lining the floor of the kitchen of this New England salt-box house are laid in a traditional zigzag pattern, and were manufactured locally in the 1750s. The earth tones are picked up in the Colonial red on the door and staircase.

mortar to hold bricks and stones together and as a rendered surface—roughcast or dashed by throwing a mixture of rocks or gravel onto wet cement with a trowel or made to resemble masonry construction by adding incised lines. From the 19th century these facades were colorwashed with distemper or covered with oil paint, although when left plain they provide a fitting backdrop for the flowers, trees, and shrubs of the surrounding landscape. If used for floors or walls, cement also furnishes a modern country-house interior with a cool, clean setting in which to celebrate punctuations of a brightly colored upholstered chair or the soft, warm honey-colored hues found in architectural features such as a wooden ceiling beam or door frame.

In its plastic state, plaster—a powdered substance formed from clay, gypsum, or lime—can be used for molding and casting, as well as being roughly troweled onto walls in random directions, then colored or colorwashed to create a timeworn country-style finish. Clay, the most ancient and widely used form of plaster, requires little processing save the addition of plant or animal fiber—to reduce shrinkage as it dries—and an organic plasticizer, traditionally natural substances such

as blood or dung. Stronger than clay, gypsum plaster sets more rapidly and can be used as both render and mortar, although as it is slightly water soluble. Its use in temperate climates is usually confined to interior decoration, as a finish for walls and ceilings.

Popular in Europe, lime plasters—created by heating limestone to high temperatures over a long period of time—have traditionally been used both outside and inside, although their long setting time of several months can delay the decoration of walls or ceilings with paint or wallpaper. Lime plaster is naturally weak and prone to shrinkage and cracking, so additives—among them sand, stone dust, animal hair, tallow, linseed, marble powder, sour milk, or wine—were traditionally incorporated into the mix to increase strength and water resistance or to allow for the rendering of delicate detail. Plain plaster surfaces were customarily painted using distemper, while oil-based paints or the fresco technique—where pigments are added to the plaster during the setting process—frequently have been favored for exterior stucco.

A fine companion for both wood and stone, plasterwork—whether left in its natural state or colored with pigments, covering walls and ceilings, or adding fine decorative detail to architectural moldings, a fireplace surround or a dado rail—lends color, texture, and a timeworn dimension to a country house dwelling.

Opposite From the red-ocher pigment on the walls reflecting the local terra-cotta tiles to the ancient beam construction to the 19th-century painted bench, this Tuscan farmhouse designed by Piero Castellini Baldissera is rooted in its historic tradition.

COLOR PALETTE The warmth and depth of the Tuscan palette, with its rusts, terra-cottas, and vivid sunshine yellows, is universally recognized.

Lemon

Corn

Sienna

As well as being the source of visionary and poetic perceptions of country color, nature also provides the colors themselves, in the guise of natural dyes and pigments that have been applied to country walls for centuries.

paint and pigments

The celebration of color is the essence of country style. The treatment of walls and woodwork gives voice to the country aesthetic, and provides the backdrop for country-inspired bed drapes, blankets, and coverlets, for kitchen tablecloths and napkins as well as earthenware plates, bowls, and cups.

The fashions born of necessity that dictated the taste for decorating the bedrooms, living rooms, and kitchens of country interiors in years gone by continue to be embraced in modern interpretations of the country-house

aesthetic—from a clean, cool, and modern high-rise apartment located in the center of Manhattan to a secluded and tiny thatch-roofed cottage in the Cotswolds or a stucco ranch-style dwelling located in the heart of Mexico. The perception of color remains key in a home proudly defined by the natural beauty and colors found in the surrounding hills and valleys, in the mountains and fields, and in the flowers, trees, and plants of the countryside. Among the most successful and authentic ways of bringing in the landscape, as well as the time-honored tradition of

Left Traditionally in Morocco walls have been coated with *tadelakt* (a smooth-marble-like finish made from sand and quicklime.) The walls in this Marrakesh house designed by Karl Fournier and Olivier Marty of Studio KO take on the natural color of the desert sands.

Opposite and Below This modern home, built by Silvio Rech and Lesley Carstens, has its roots in the mud huts or *rondavels* of Southern African vernacular building. The rich textures and tones resonate from the straw and mud walls.

enlivening an interior with color, is colorwashing, whereby the age-old technique of limewashing or whitewashing is given a new and highly original look by the addition of colored pigments.

The technique of limewashing walls dates back to 8000BC when the walls of small huts inhabited by the poor were decorated to emulate the sumptuous dwellings of the rich. Excavations of Neolithic sites in Turkey, Babylonia, and Greece reveal the rich heritage of this venerable practise. Later ages adopted the refinement of adding color to the limewash to form a colorwash, to add variety and vibrancy to decoration.

Limewash is an ancient paint made from limestone which has been crushed, burnt, and slaked with water to make lime putty. The lime putty is matured for several months before being thinned with water to make limewash. Limewash is naturally white and forms a complex crystalline matrix which has a matte, slightly chalky appearance. It can be colored with pigments and be applied internally or externally, where it works best on porous surfaces such as a traditional lime plaster, lime render, stone, and brick. Unlike modern barrier paints,

Mud

Tobacco

COLOR PALETTE Strong earth colors can be accentuated by stark white upholstery or complemented by natural pig-skin and cottons.

Calico

Peanut

Egg Yolk

COLOR PALETTE The
warm earth tones of ocher
and umber can be enlivened
by the use of strong reds and
pattern or kept cooler by
off-whites and beiges.

limewash works by sinking into the surface. It hardens
by absorbing carbon dioxide from the atmosphere to
form crystals of calcium carbonate, which give the
limewash its distinctive appearance and protective
qualities. When used on porous surfaces, the color will
deepen if there is any dampness in the background
material, hence its attractive and characteristic shading.

Tallow (animal fat) or raw linseed oil are traditional
additives which help to improve its water-shedding
qualities when used externally. As it is a water-based
paint, limewash is not easily absorbed into less porous
surfaces, such as cement renders or hard gypsum plasters,
and therefore it won't wear nearly as well on these bases.
Additives such as casein (skim milk) can be added
to help it bond to these less porous materials. Even new
plasterwork limewashed in this way is imbued with the
appearance of gentle weathering over time by the natural
elements such as the wind, the rain, and the sun.

Above The tri-partite display of
colorwash in the *piano nobile*
(first floor main reception
room) in this grand Tuscan
farmhouse is used to visually
decrease the height of the
15-foot ceiling. Dark beige is
used below, a sand color above,
and off-white is the freize.

Opposite Originally a stable,
this Tuscan drawing room
designed by Piero Castellini
Baldissera retains its exposed
vaulted ceiling made of local
brick. The walls are painted
with a yellow-ocher distemper
colorwash. The natural tones
are further heightened by the
sisal rugs on the floor and
the ocher and reds in the
furnishing fabrics.

COLOR PALETTE Off-
whites, creams, and lemons
with a broken-color finish
allow for simple, natural-
colored fabrics, but also
provide a backdrop for a
more vibrant approach.

Linen

Sunbeam

Below The sponged plaster
off-white walls in this Belgian
home create a peaceful Zen-like
atmosphere in this essentially
oriental interior. A relaxed
neutral canvas like this can
be created by a wheat
colorwash on the walls.

Above In the main salon of this
country house in the Dordogne
the walls have a sophisticated
colorwash finish. Three tones
of warm off-white are utilized
to create a depth of color and
texture, which is picked up in
the fabrics and furnishings.

Opposite In this 18th-century
Tuscan farmhouse designed by
Ilaria Miani, the structure of brick
floor and beams with exposed
terra-cotta tiles above is softened
by the gentle yellow colorwash
on the walls and painted plum
baseboard. The multi-colored
fabrics also soften the appearance.

The pigments used to transform limewash from its
naturally white state can be either natural or, increasingly
in more recent times, manufactured. The natural
pigments are clay and silica, colored with iron oxides
in the earth. They are mined all over the world but
some take their names from their primary locations—
Siena and Umbria, for instance. Natural pigments have
less coloring intensity than manufactured pigments,
which are produced mainly from iron oxides to replicate
traditional earth pigments. These are stronger in hue,
consistent, and extremely durable.

From the earth were born the oldest colors of all,
including ocher and umber from clay, while animals and
vegetables have yielded mellow and sumptuous hues
such as rich madder, indigo, and cochineal from crushed
beetles. For centuries, earth pigments have been a ready
source of inexpensive color for water- as well as oil-based
paints that have traditionally been favored for the
decoration of the plaster and wooden surfaces—both
inside and out—of simple country-style houses.

The colors that decorate a country house are dictated
by the surrounding landscape. Paints originating from

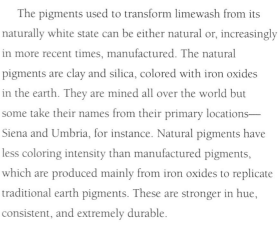

Left In this small salon in the Dordogne, the walls are painted with a pale yellow colorwash, which accentuates the neutral rush mat and the limewood ceiling. These bring into focus the plum fabric on the 18th-century chairs and fabric screen.

Opposite In the same house, in the grand salon, a deep yellow colorwash is punctuated by the solid green of the bookcases and textured and patterned fabrics. In this home all the rooms and hallways are painted in different shades of yellow, from very pale lemon to deep saturated gold.

local clays, soils, and plants forge a visual bond between a dwelling and the neighboring countryside. Until the 19th century, most paints were derived from earth pigments, while fabrics were printed with muted vegetable dyes. This dependable palette included tones ranging from off-white, gray, and buff to terra-cotta, red, and green.

A range of some fifteen fairly dependable inorganic pigments were available to a painter by the end of the 16th century. These original colors were obtained from three distinct sources: ochers, umbers, and other earths that had been in use since earliest times; crushed semi-precious stones including lapis lazuli and azurite, green malachite, and yellow orpiment for the brightest hues; and a few synthetic pigments produced by simple chemistry, such as vermilion, blue smalt, green verdigris, lead white, red lead, and lead tin yellow. Logwood black and cochineal red were among the new colors introduced from the Americas, along with more plentiful supplies of brazilwood and indigo.

Venice long played host to the Western pigment trade. Exotic and intense colors—such as pure blue derived from the costly mineral lapis lazuli, azurite, yellow gamboge, and red lac from the East—tended to be rare and very expensive by the time they reached the far corners of Europe. One of the most significant changes to revolutionize the range of the color menu was the invention of Prussian blue at the beginning of the 18th century. A deep blue synthetic pigment, this cheap and reliable colorant replaced high-priced minerals and could be used in large amounts. Strong and stable greens became a possibility for the first time.

Dating to prehistoric times, pigments procured from earths rich in iron oxides are among the oldest sources of colors for artists and decorators. These include ocher, sienna—which ranges from yellow-brown to reddish orange tones—and umbers that tend to be brown in color due to a high amount of manganese dioxide. When

Honey

Nectar

COLOR PALETTE The tones of off-whites and yellows work particularly well with strong doses of reds and greens.

43

heated to a high temperature, these juicy pigments become richer and darker and are then referred to as burnt ocher, burnt sienna, and burnt umber.

The spectrum of earth pigments include a variety of red tones, occasionally referred to as the red ochers, and black from magnetite, yellow from limonite, brown from siderite, and dark brown from pyrites. Standing alongside these natural examples are iron oxide pigments that have been synthetically produced, including reds that range from light Turkey red to dark Indian reds and Venetian red. Rich in minerals, especially red iron oxides, Italy has been an important source of earth pigments for both artists and decorators for centuries.

Various types of vegetable matter have also been instrumental for coloring paints and fabrics prior to the introduction of synthetic aniline dyes in the mid-19th century. These include madder, a red pigment extracted

Frost Blue

Sea

Lichen

COLOR PALETTE Choosing blues and greens creates a cool, restful ambience, particularly with lighter shades.

Crocus   Coral

COLOR PALETTE Tones of lavender and pink combine
to create a light, playful ambiance

from the root of the plant *Rubia tinctorum;* quercitron,
which is derived from the inner bark of a species of oak
that makes luscious shades of yellow ranging from
marigold to daffodil; the blue pigment indigo from the
leaves of the plant genus *Indigofera*; and woad, a gray-blue
shade. Supplementing vegetable dyes were those crushed
or squeezed from small living creatures, cochineal,
kermes, and murex shellfish. All three were able to
produce strong, rich scarlets and purple hues.

Rapid developments in 19th-century technology paved
the way to purifying metal ores, resulting in an explosion
of new pigments: brilliant yellows, reds, and oranges

based on cadmium; chrome yellows and greens; cobalt
blues and greens; zinc, barium, and strontium yellows;
and French ultramarine. The debut of these inorganic
tints more than trebled the range of pigments previously
available, and introduced colors of unparalleled intensity
and clarity. They were matched at the end of the century
by a set of synthetic organic colors that expanded the
red and purple tones available.

For centuries, we have turned to the minerals of the
earth, the trees, plants, flowers, and berries, small
animals and insects found in the surrounding landscape
for inspiration in decorating country houses. From
the golden ochers and rich, earthy terra-cottas covering
the stucco walls of a Tuscan villa to the delicate pinks
and pale blues of roses and harebells that outline the
white wooden paneling of a farmhouse nestled in the
Swedish countryside, the natural colors of the earth
have yielded a spectrum of hues. They bring life and
color to the country home as well as attending to
practical needs—the desire to keep cool in a hot and
sultry climate and the longing for a sense of comfort and
warmth in an isolated cottage nestled in frosty terrain.

Opposite and Left The lavender-
blue distemper colorwash is
inspired by the lavender growing
in abundance in the Tuscan
countryside. It can be used in
solid wall covering or with off-
white to create a striped effect.
Here it is accented with the
pale-pink-and-rose striped
ticking on the sofa and chair.

Above In another Tuscan house
a rose-and-beige striped ticking
on the daybed is this time
complemented by a warm sienna
colorwash on the walls.

the color palettes

cool colors

A PALETTE OF COOL COLORS has long been a fundamental component of country-house architecture. Pale colors speak to the simplicity and naturalness that are the essential ingredients of the rural tradition, while at the same time lending elegance and grandeur to the rustic interior. Structural features including walls, ceilings, floors, doors, and staircases, and even furniture colored with cool mellow shades of cream, yellow, green, or blue, create the comforting and relaxing atmosphere that lies at the heart of country style.

From New England to Provence, the rooms of a country dwelling look to the surrounding countryside for a palette of hues that will feel welcoming. Brimming with a host of subtle variations of a single hue—the yellow of primroses, straw, or lemons; the green of olives, mint, or grass, for example—nature's landscape offers up a harmony of cool refreshing shades that bring sanctuary and solace to a bedroom, a sitting room, or a terrace.

Light-hued, muted color schemes for country interiors tend to look to gentle landscape colors for inspiration, such as milky yellows, ivories, olive greens, pale blues, and soft grays. Georgian decorators mixed a variety of cool off-white colors by adding measures of black or blue to white. Today the tradition of using off-whites, various tones of gray, and other stone colors favored in the early 18th century for the plastered and softwood-paneled walls of Georgian interiors remains a popular choice for a modern country dwelling. Light and airy painted decoration, set against a backdrop of pale scrubbed floorboards and punctuated with delicate painted furniture, are the crucial elements of Scandinavian country style. Warmth is frequently brought into the mix of the cool palette with accents, such as the blues, soft and dusty grays, and rose pinks found in Scandinavian color schemes.

Cool colors are not confined to northern climes, for in countries that take pleasure in hot weather all year round, Morocco, Mexico, and Spain, for example, pale hues that reflect the warm sand and dust of the parched desert proffer a welcome and refreshing refuge from the sizzling heat by calming the intense and vivid greens and blazing vermilions found in the surrounding landscape. Clean and elegant—whether slick and sharp modern or looking back to the past—a light, cool color palette brings a reasuring calm to the country-house interior.

Opposite, from top Muted cool colors create a calm and tranquil Long Island sitting room.

The wooden extension to this Connecticut Federal stone house is painted matte gray to mirror the colors of the local fieldstone.

Whites and off-whites bring a serene atmosphere to this guest bedroom in the eaves of a Belgian country home.

The stark white of the fireplace and expansive walls offset this Tuscan terrazzo floor.

The brown and white stripes on the blinds of this Tuscan dining room are mirrored in the simple painted chairs.

Pure white walls and bed linen accentuate the lines of these 19th-century French beds.

Previous pages The earth colors, so prevalent in the Tuscan countryside, are evident in the old terra-cotta tiles on the floor, the warm yellow-ochre distemper wash on the walls and the terra-cotta linen of the dining chairs in this Tuscan house designed by Piero Castellini Baldissera.

The ancient color white is at once ordinary, yet powerful and dynamic, cool and clean. It creates a mood of quiet and serenity, of relaxation and restfulness—qualities that lie at the heart of the country-house ethic.

whites and off-whites

Right In this converted 1960s schoolhouse in Tuscany designed by Mimmi O'Connell, the orient blends seamlessly with the Tuscan interior. The matte white creates the perfect canvas for the mix of comfortable sofas with lacquer boxes and 19th-century Chinese scholar's chairs.

Right below In the same room the matte white on the walls and bookcase is in stark contrast to the local multi-colored terrazzo floor and the dramatic pair of 18th-century Indonesian carved wooden riders from the island of Floris.

Opposite In a room designed by Ilaria Miani, the off-white walls allow space for the subtle gradation of colors in the furnishings, from the metal beds to the striped Nobilis curtains and muted floral bedspreads by Nina Campbell.

Refreshingly simple, white creates the ideal canvas upon which a variety of colors and textures can be layered. The sumptuous, vivid hues of Indian textiles or Berber carpets are intensified when set against a whitewashed stucco wall or pale, scrubbed floorboards. White allows the rich, bright colors of fabrics or the mellow warmth of honey-colored wooden floors, doors, or ceiling beams to take center stage in a kitchen, sitting room, or bath.

When used alone as a feature of a country-style dwelling white is versatile and expressive. Depending on the quality of light from the surrounding landscape—the cold, harsh light of the Swedish countryside, the cool, gray light of rural Maine, or the sun-drenched glow of the Provençal countryside—white reflects the character of the surrounding landscape. It plays a key role in enhancing space, as well as in the illumination of a room. Faded whites that have acquired a lovely patina with use and age are central to the country style, such as aged whitewashed stucco walls, old wooden paneling painted in a creamy hue, worn pearl-gray floor tiles, nubbly fabrics the color of snow used on a well-loved chair, or a window curtain bleached by the rays of the sun.

Simplicity is key. An interior decorated with a harmony of pure whites is cool and tranquil, a serene and contemplative space. White amplifies space and accentuates natural light. There are many different shades of white and its near relative, gray. The traditional soft, dirty whites—the beautiful mellow whites of distemper, milk paints, limewash, and whitewash—age well and suit the faded character of well-worn wood and old fabric.

Whether cloudy or clear, ashen or grayish in tone, the countless variations of white are determined by the

Pure White

Owl

Stone

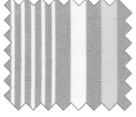

COLOR PALETTE Whites
and off-whites provide the
perfect backdrop for fabric
accessories: cool textured
cottons, pale florals, and
complementary stripes.

sunlight and shade from the surrounding landscape and the color of structural features—the pale softness of a stone fireplace, the warm rich patina of a weathered oak door, or the spicy reddish-brown of terra-cotta kitchen tiles.

Before 1860 these were the shades of white that prevailed. After that time, the addition of chemicals to paint mixes produced a bright, pure, dense white that brought both a dramatic intensity and clarity that proved especially ideal for the decoration during the Art Deco and Modernist periods.

White lightens the tonal value when added to a primary color—red, blue, and yellow—or secondary colors created by mixing two primaries. The tones created by combining progressively lighter tints, which result from adding greater and greater quantities of white, can give a room a timeworn feel. The practise of

Opposite Every element blends beautifully to create a tranquil environment in this Long Island, New York home by Tricia Foley; from the off-whites to the subtle grays to the 19th-century fruitwood table, the sisal mat, and the collections of glass and creamware.

Above The choice of bright white on the walls of this Tuscan home allows the ornate bed architecture to dominate while retaining a crisp and cool environment.

Right In Upstate New York tones of blue-gray cover the walls of this late 18th-century home. The planks on the left are original to the house, those on the right are 50 years old.

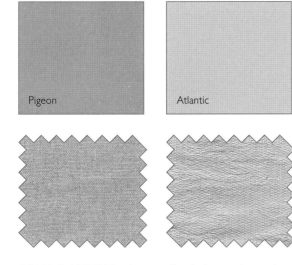

| Pigeon | Atlantic |

COLOR PALETTE The elegance of cool whites and neutrals is enhanced by the addition of linens in soft tones of stone and steel.

colorwashing or the adding of limewash to pigments gives new plasterwork the appearance of soft weathering by both time and sun. The gentle, rich colors of milk paint—traditionally applied as a flat coat to everything from walls to furniture—possess the mellow beauty brought about by the passing years. An especially effective method for achieving the soft and luminous country look is achieved by combining various shades of one color—such as yellow or terra-cotta.

Often overlooked as a color, white shows all other colors to their best advantage and adds freshness to almost any hue. When combined with a selection of bold and intense primary colors, or with its classic partner black, white achieves the modern simplicity of a Mondrian painting. Green and white are a natural partnership, delicate and countrified. White walls give a room a cool, relaxing, and refreshing atmosphere when united with mellow greens of the trees, plants, and flowers of the garden. This combination brings the surrounding landscape into the country house interior.

The traditional pairing of blue and white is a familiar and highly appealing one for the country dwelling. It is perhaps the most popular of all color combinations. The blue and white pairing can be found in a check gingham tablecloth, tiles, countless varieties of

COLOR PALETTE White and off-white and natural materials are always excellent partners. Here natural wood, rush, wicker, and linens blend seamlessly.

Peace

Buttermilk

Lotus

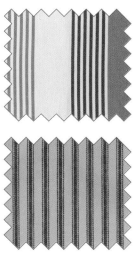

Left, above Simplicity is all. The white of the walls and woodwork and the natural beiges and taupes combined with the strong wood tones of original 18th-century floorboards make a country sanctuary in Connecticut.

Left, center The stark white walls, kitchen cabinets, and table and chairs, with sections of stainless steel, complement the original wide mellow-toned elm floorboards in this 18th-century Connecticut house. Reflective surfaces have always been important in country homes, to maximize light in rooms in which windows were kept small to keep houses warm in winter and cool in summer.

Left, below The white walls, tiles, and cabinets in the kitchen of this lodge in the mountains of Norway allow the wood of the floorboards, the massive 19th-century oak pedestal table, and the set of English Windsor chairs to stand out.

Opposite The use of a white background will always give extra emphasis to the furnishings in a room. Here the 19th-century pine farmhouse table, wicker chairs, and linen drapes dominate the color palette chosen by designer Nicolette Schouten.

sanctuary from the sizzling heat, sand, and intense colors found in the arid landscape. In similar fashion houses in the frigid temperatures of Scandinavia look to a cool, muted palette of pale timeworn colors—white and off-white, clotted cream, vanilla, and pearl gray—to bring serenity into the interior and enhance the brief daylight. Following in the footsteps of the Gustavian tradition, white walls and wall paneling are typically punctuated with outlines in the soft shades of the local flora—the green of leaves, the yellow-green of grasses, the washed browns of the earth, the pale pink of roses, and the light blue of harebells. Warmth is enhanced by the addition of deep, rich hues that keep the crisp, cold temperatures of the outside world at bay.

Whether tempering the fierce heat of a blazing sun in Portugal or bringing translucent light into a cottage in Norway, across the globe white has many places in the decoration of a country interior—from crockery to curtains, marble fireplaces to the tiles paving a veranda.

Left Swedish country style is about "ice" colors, whites and off-whites. They blend seamlessly with the ancient terra-cotta bricks and natural pine.

Opposite In a central Tuscan farmhouse, a pale gray rough plaster wall has an off-white floral stencil on a beige background with rust and off-white banding bordered by a darker gray.

Below This hallway in southern France shows two distinct influences; that of the light and warmth of Provence and the cool of owner Anna Bonde's native Sweden. The neutral tones of the rough plastered walls, local stone floors, and furnishings are complemented by the sympathetic use of old fabrics.

everyday crockery, and mattress ticking. This classic color combination looks to the 17th century when vast quantities of Chinese porcelain began arriving across Europe via the cargo ships of the East India companies. A humble but nonetheless eye-catching match, blue and white gives a homespun feel to an interior, especially when mixed up and layered in a host of lively textile patterns including spots, stripes, and checks.

White domesticates the color red, just as it brings an unpretentious and homely character when combined with blues and greens. The cheerful, light-hearted freshness of red-and-white check gingham, calico, or striped fabrics is irresistible and synonymous with hospitality, while textiles and crockery boasting red and white combinations of toile de Jouy patterns in soft madder red are more sophisticated and refined.

The color white plays an important role in the decoration of a country dwelling in cold, frosty climates and in areas that enjoy hot weather all year round as well. In Spain, Morocco, Arizona, and Mexico, bright white shares the stage with pale dry shades—light terra-cottas, buffs, and soft butter yellows—affording a refreshing

Dillweed

Mink

Dusty Pink

COLOR PALETTE The
perception of whites and off-
whites can be changed
dramatically by the use of
accent fabrics such as cool
cottons or linens in pure
white or in warm stripes
or florals.

In the pursuit of simplicity and comfort—which are essential features of country-style living—pale, cool colors used on expanses of walls, or as floor coverings and furnishing textiles, add elegance and serenity to any country-style interior.

creams and pale yellows

Above The pale yellow walls of this Dordogne kitchen are warmed by the terra-cotta tiles and 19th-century provincial French mahogany furniture.

Above right and Opposite Architect Gilles Pellerin chose cool creams for the walls of his Provençal house to throw into focus the reclaimed chestnut boards, 18th-century stripped doors, and carefully chosen artwork. The wall color blends with the ceiling beams and table.

Moving away from off-whites, suggestion of color can be introduced into an interior with shades of creams and the palest yellows. These shades still fall within the cool palette, but their spectrum covers a range of slightly more dominant tones. They are unsurpassed in their ability to bring freshness and a sense of calm to living rooms, bedrooms, and kitchens alike.

Pigments mixed with milk paint, limewash, or distemper take the harsh chill away from pure white. Subtle and appealing, a spectrum of the soft natural hues

COLOR PALETTE Cool creams and pale yellows are complemented by simple linens in neutral tones for a more sophisticated look. Alternatively, a more "cozy" look can be achieved with checks and stripes.

Oatmeal

Sherbet

Tallow

Vanilla

Red Earth

COLOR PALETTE Creams and pale yellows create a harmonious ambience which can be further enhanced by linens in taupes and other natural colors.

Above In this Upstate New York cottage the cream wall color is accented by the terra-cotta baseboard and architrave. The 19th-century ladder-back chair is similarly painted.

Opposite The architectural features—the wide wooden boards, ceiling beams, and stone fireplace—are the main focal points in this pale yellow room. Bleaching the floorboards gives a cool-toned finish to the wood.

Right Almost every surface in the planked kitchen/dining area of this cabin in the Oslo fjord is painted a neutral cream to create a cool, calming effect: the ceiling, floor, walls, and cabinets. The 19th-century table and painted chairs are softened by the use of red and pink tones in the fabrics and in the transferware crockery.

found in nature—primrose, beige, buff, driftwood, pale ocher, clotted cream, pannacotta, and goat's cheese—in a wealth of distinct tones and delicate nuances of color, have long been favored for the decoration of a country-style interior. Bleached by sun and sea, the sandy colors of northern sea coasts comprise a naturally harmonious color palette. Readily obtainable from earth pigments such as ochers and umbers are the widely used buffs and browns. Because white can be so cold, umber brings something slightly warmer into milk paint, while still remaining in the cool range. In the 18th and 19th centuries the well-named "drab" was a popular color for the decoration of the Georgian house interior, as were the gray and cream shades evocative of weathered stone.

One of the three primary colors, yellow—cheerful and full of life, the color of sunlight, daffodils, butter, lemons, and gold—captivates as a glowing and uplifting shade. Luminous and radiant, yellow lightens and brightens the interior of any room in a country-style house, its ebullient spirit encouraging a comfortable and hospitable atmosphere. The addition of white or brown tints makes an intense yellow pigment cool and serene. Pale primrose, sun-bleached straw, and faded ocher not only warm up walls, but

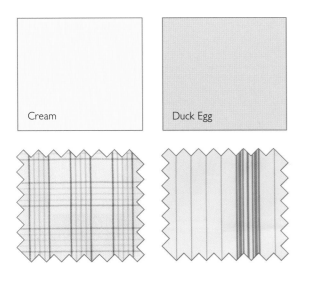

Cream

Duck Egg

Right In Swedish country style the inside reflects the light of the exterior. Every surface is painted, including the walls, the dining furniture, and the distinctive 18th-century clock.

Below Even in Mexico cool shades can be used as a contrast to the brightness and starkness of the exterior light.

Opposite With the pale cream walls, plain-white-linen sofa and footstool, and off-white woodwork, the accents of blue catch the eye; from the cushions and Jane Churchill fabric to the blue-painted chair with blue-and-white ticking.

COLOR PALETTE Cobalt blue has historically been a favorite pigment for decorating everything from ceramics to glass to fabrics. It is particularly successful when teamed with creams and pale yellows, often in stripes and check fabrics.

also work well with various shades of gray and white. Cool, pale yellows add brilliant highlights to wooden wall paneling. The application of a variety of tones of a single color, such as yellow, can be especially effective with different shades applied to different sections of a wall creating a soft, luminous impression.

The Gustavian palette—consisting of timeworn clotted creams, ivory, vanilla, and washed browns punctuated by leaf greens, pale grays, pinks, and blues found in local flora—has been traditionally favored for the decoration of cottages located in cooler regions of the world, such as Sweden or the northern reaches of England or Germany, for example. The subtle shades of ocher and yellow bring a mellow character to the walls of country villas in hotter climates, such as Tuscany, Califronia, or Mexico. White walls, floors of pale maple or bleached walnut or painted beige punctuated with black detailing gives a sharp modern edge to a country-style dwelling anywhere, from New York to Barcelona, and from Cuba to Prague.

Color schemes based on natural hues are by definition clean, simple, and straightforward, yet creams and pale yellows need not be dull or unsophisticated. An assortment of textures adds depth, interest, and a pleasing variety to a muted color range. Such textures may take the form of

earthenware crockery lining the mantelpiece of a kitchen hearth, or pine floorboards painted or scrubbed a pale mellow gold, or a floor covered with quarry tiles, slate, bamboo, sisal, or woven rush mats. Limed oak cupboards, granite, or marble tabletops, windows hung with calico or muslin curtains, wickerwork or cane, woven leather or waxed wooden chairs left plain or covered with raw linens and silks—all are materials that evoke the country.

In an even more refined application of natural colors, architectural details, such as cornicing or plasterwork, are picked out in a range of narrowly differentiated shades—a decorative technique that found favor in the grand Georgian houses of the 18th century. With the rays of sun streaming through the windows, the cool buff shade of natural plaster appears soft, luminous, and ultimately tranquil. At night by candlelight, it springs to life. Such neutral tones, embracing but not enclosing, create an atmosphere of space and light.

The antithesis of vivid, saturated tones, natural colors are shown to best advantage on their own or in subtle gradations of closely related shades. But this is hardly a limitation, as there remains variety and depth within the palette of neutrals and the addition of texture broadens the range even further. Crisp, pure white ceilings and woodwork enhance walls or floors painted in warm, creamy whites and yellows or pale, muddied shades of brown. The bright strong colors that boast not only an earthy quality, but also partner well with natural shades include brick, Indian reds, and warm indigo blues, which will not overpower the fundamental softness of these wonderfully cool, pale colors.

Lemon Ice

Off-Black

Left The inner hallway of this 1754 house in Connecticut retains its original structure. Drama is added to the pale yellow walls and white paneling and banisters by the matte brown painted stair treads and painted boards.

Opposite and Far Left In this manor house in Normandy, designed by Dominique Kieffer, the pale yellow walls with dark woodwork allow for a dramatic statement. The 19th-century metal campaign beds are softened with natural fabric edged in black.

Below In Normandy the pale yellow kitchen walls are dominated by the strongly graphic brown and black striped blind, the old pine *atelier* table, the brushed steel appliances, and the steel 1930's chairs topped with simple black cushions.

COLOR PALETTE Creams and pale yellows can be given a dramatic overhaul when combined with heavy linens in blacks and dark grays striped with beige or taupe.

When considering a cool color palette, green immediately springs to mind. Across the globe green is the color of the landscape, of trees and grass. The linchpin of the garden, it is a foil for the eye-catching colors of flowers and fruit.

greens

Willow

Gray-Green

Lavender

COLOR PALETTE Green, particularly in its lighter tones, evokes restfulness and harmony. Use it as a solid color on woodwork and as a broken color on walls.

A host of luscious shades makes up the greens of nature, ranging from the deep dark fir green of spruce trees to the bright yellow green of new growth in springtime, from the silvery green of rosemary and sage to the sumptuous rich emerald of fresh new turf. Green shows itself in a broad variety of shades—pistachio, olive, and mint, grass, ivy, moss, and leaf, apple and lime, the color of peas and seaweed, celery and lettuce, of emeralds, frogs, parrots, and the sea. Refreshing and spirited, green celebrates the flora and fauna of nature and takes the palm as the color which above all others enjoys a light, cool, and restful reputation.

In all of its many incarnations, green has held forth as one of the most ubiquitous of colors for interior decoration over the centuries, with particular shades identified with distinctive periods or styles. For example, the deep, rich green of pine trees was a favored hue for Georgian paneling, bright pea green became fashionable in the later 18th century, a yellowish green was preferred for a Federal interior, while a vivid,

Left The pale green colorwash on the walls reflects the Tuscan hills surrounding the farmhouse. This is powerfully emphasized by the strong matte green shutters. These colors are off-set by the original terra-cotta tiles and the 19th-century two-tone off-white painted table and stacking chairs.

Opposite In a bedroom of the same house, designed by Piero Castellini Baldissera, the distressed green colorwash above dado and distressed gray below create a perfect setting for the elaborate 19th-century French cast-iron bed. The bed is further accentuated by the lilac headboard and throw.

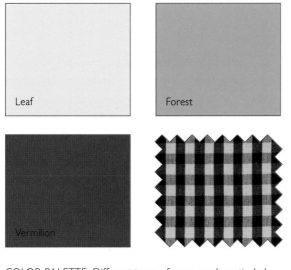

Leaf

Forest

Vermilion

COLOR PALETTE Different tones of green work particularly well together, and with the darker tones of polished wood. It also complements wood painted in Colonial red. Fabrics with strong checks in cream and black can take a riot of greens.

Ceramic tiles in a menu of green colors bring a cool, clean atmosphere to country dwellings located in hot climates from Casablanca to Santa Fe.

Green can also bring a sense of refined elegance and sophistication to a country interior. In 18th-century Britain, the architect Robert Adam made use of a variety of defining shades of light greens and blue greens for finely modeled architectural features such as dado rails, fireplace surrounds, and moldings. The jade greens and celadons of the East associated with the porcelains of the Sung dynasty, as well as the Neoclassical greens favored by Adam and his contemporaries, tend to be soft and delicate, evocative of gentility and taste and the luxurious grandeur of a stately home.

The color green shares a special connection with Nordic interiors. The style of the traditional Scandinavian country dwelling has in large part been determined by the surrounding countryside—the abundant timber forests,

Opposite From the 18th century, Robert Adams' "pea-green" was a favorite choice for both living rooms and bedrooms. It is used in this house in Long Island, designed by Naomi Leff.

Below In Columbia County, New York, the dining room has been painted in traditional style with local scenes. In the 18th and 19th centuries itinerant painters would travel around accepting commissions from house owners. The colors used are traditional, as are the accented terra-cotta or ox-blood colored doors.

brilliant green enjoyed wide support for the decoration of rooms in the Empire style. Victorian taste tended to lean toward dull greens and olive shades, with the late 19th century Arts and Crafts movement particularly identified with a dusky, vegetable green.

Easy on the eyes, green has long been used in interiors for many purposes, from colored panels and woodwork to textiles and furnishings. A room decorated all in shades of green could never be considered humdrum or incompatible. Just as a wide variety of green hues mingle together across the natural landscape, most shades of green—from spruce to sea green and emerald to pistachio—harmonize effortlessly for bedcovers, throws, quilts, and blankets. A contemplative color, employed traditionally for the walls of a library or study, green in all its shades lends an air of rest and relaxation to living rooms and bedrooms as well, although it is most peaceful and perhaps most versatile in subtle muted shades. Delicate and countrified, the natural partnership of cool green and white works especially well, and is frequently used in bold graphic checks or flower patterns for table linens, upholstery, pillows, and bedspreads.

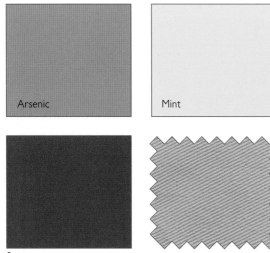

Arsenic

Mint

Storm

COLOR PALETTE Soft tones of green can be used in either a modern or period room. An extremely adaptable color, it can sooth or excite. Solid, strong fabrics can subtly add another dimension to the overall feel of the palette.

Above Large blocks of strong cool color can be softened by the addition of a lighter tone, as with the chair fabric. The use of the dark gray trim and white "baseboard" serves to create color panels which further enhance the cool ambience.

Left The matte forest green of the walls reflects the verdant Tuscan countryside. The dark gray border and white panels add extra drama and clean modernity.

Below left In this Moroccan bathroom, hand-made tiles with inherent variations in color and texture create a modulating blue-green fish-scale effect.

Opposite The main salon of this early 19th-century coaching inn in northern France has rough plaster walls and original beams painted a distressed icy green. The artist owner, Julie Prisca, was inspired by frost in the landscape.

lakes, and mountains coupled with the severe climate of long harsh winters. To keep the harsh cold temperatures at bay, farmhouse cabins tend to be built low into the terrain. Green grasses and lichen blanketing the roofs supply natural heating and further merge the house with the landscape. Timeworn and faded greenwood paneling and rough-hewn logs painted a soft green bring the mellow colors of the rural environment inside. Brightly colored scatter rugs and throw pillows add warmth to the frosty, clear palette of a Gustavian interior.

Pale muted shades of green used over large surface areas can bring a cool and airy quality to an interior, while stronger tints add a lively touch to smaller details and structural features, such as a door frame, a fireplace surround, a staircase, or ceiling beams. Subtle tonalities borrowed from the flower garden or hedgerows—russet red, golden yellow, or rose pink—combined with willow, fir, or lime green lend a room decorated in country style a comfortable rustic expression. Spicy combinations of lime and saffron or mango magnify

Rich Jade

Folly

Olive

Grass

the light to brighten and energize the surrounding space. Dark forest green, boldly used, brings a cheerful, folk-art spirit when married with a tomato red.

The greens that decorate the country interior have traditionally originated in the surrounding landscape and vegetation. The fields and hills of England bring weathered gray-greens and dull faded shades into a stone cottage nestled in the Cotswolds, a rustic farmhouse in Connecticut looks to the timber-rich forests for bright saturated greens, walls lined with tin-glazed terra-cotta tiles in sage green add a cool refuge from the sizzling heat in a Marrakesh villa. Green is cool; green is calm; green is the color of country.

Above, far left Green is a traditional color used in living rooms and bedrooms. It provides an excellent platform for antique furniture and ceramics, in this case creamware.

Above left In the bedroom of an 18th-century house in Columbia County, New York, the solid green paint is Farrow and Ball's Card Room Green.

Below The play of the hydrangea green alternating with white panels on the walls of this Tuscan bedroom, by Ilaria Miani, is drawn together with the use of the dramatically striped Nobilis fabric.

COLOR PALETTE Green is an excellent and obvious color for garden rooms and conservatories, as well as interiors. Here floral fabrics work, whereas in a more modern setting a dominant stripe with contrasting colors is equally successful.

Opposite Cool colors can successfully bring the outside in, as in this conservatory in Connecticut by Champalimaud Design. The off-white painted-clapboard exterior wall and Greek Revival door surround are accentuated by the Dutch door painted sage green. This combination continues with the cushions on the bench and 19th-century wrought-iron chairs.

Cool blues are associated with northern climes and with the intense but cool northern light. There are a host of shades of blue on the cool end of the spectrum, and these fresh tones engender a clean, peaceful ambience.

cool blues

Our perceptions of the color blue are highly influenced by our geography. If you were to ask a Danish person to think of blue, the color he would immediately visualise would be completely different from the mental image a Mexican, for example, would produce when posed the same question. This diversity offers two quite separate decorating styles in the country tradition. Warm blues, which include an element of red, have a very diffferent effect in an interior; see page 106 to 111.

Cool blues, which we look at in this section, are essentially Scandinavian in feel, though evident in other northern regions that share the same quality of light, such as the rest of northern Europe and the northeast coast of the U.S. Seaside themes are often associated with cool blues, and can encourage a sense of wellbeing, calm, and restfulness. Deep navy blues, calling to mind the seafaring tradition, take on a rich, happy glow in bright light, contrasting sharply with the nautical idiom that allies blue with a feeling of sadness and gloom, as in "feeling blue," which comes from the tradition of deepwater sailing ships flying a blue flag when the captain died. Cool navy blues always contain some black, unlike French navy, which has a warmer, red tone.

It is not only the quality of light that defines this range of colors. It is the natural pigment that is the starting point of all these schemes: cobalt. Derived from smalt, cobalt is incredibly stable. During the 19th century, around 70 to 80 percent of the world production of cobalt blue was produced at the Norwegian Blaafarveværket, a

COLOR PALETTE Pale cool blues are often thought of as Scandinavian colors. Certainly when associated with grays and off-whites they create a restful, clean canvas.

Winter Blue

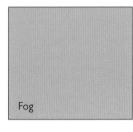

Fog

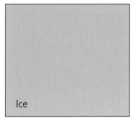

Ice

Opposite, above In an 18th-century Dutch farmhouse, the plank wall is painted matte blue gray in contrast to the cream cabinets topped with granite.

Opposite, below The solid gray blue color painted on the plank tongue-and-groove walls creates an oasis of calm in this Connecticut bathroom.

Right In a restored wooden house in Goose Creek, Long Island, the plank walls have been painted cornflower blue. With accents of stark white and dark blue, the colors reflect waterside living.

Right The pale lilac pigment on the walls reflects the lavender growing in the cottage garden of this Tuscan home. This is just a hint of color, which becomes more vibrant in the afternoon sun. The matte blue-painted low dresser and chairs, the natural wood of the farmhouse table, and the old terra-cotta tiles blend seamlessly.

Below, right This sturdy paneled door, painted a washed woad color, leads to a deeper blue wall behind and combines with the warmer, local terra-cotta tiles.

Below The original vertical planked wall in this Connecticut house built for a local dignitary in 1754 is painted with a mid-blue pigment. The late 18th-century blanket chest retains its original paint finish. These chests were often painted with ox blood.

Forget-me-not

Hyacinth

Dark blue

COLOR PALETTE From Copenhagen to Connecticut to Cheltenham, the subtle tones of the cobalt pigment gives these interiors a common heritage. The theme of blue and cool lilac can be reflected with simple colored denim fabrics.

Above In this English kitchen designed by Lena Proudlock the painted Gustavian chairs, lilac painted tabletop, and many shades of off-white and blues give a Scandinavian feel.

company which both mined and manufactured the pigment, run by the Prussian industrialist Benjamin Wegner. It is this Scandinavian history—the production of the natural substance from the region itself, and its application in decoration—that continues to give cool blues their distinctive character.

Planked walls painted in tones of icy blue evoke the Gustavian period of 18th-century Sweden. These are particularly suited to bedrooms, bathrooms, and kitchens. Looking to the landscape for inspiration, the decoration of the traditional Scandinavian farmhouse testifies to the desire to enhance all available natural light and brighten rooms throughout the long, dark winter months. Cool blues work well painted on large expanses of wood, so that planked walls, floors, cabinets, and doors can all benefit from these lighter shades. Rich blue-gray dados, doorways, and window frames punctuated with the addition of a painted blue chair, pale blue cabinet doors, or striped bed coverings and hangings bring simplicity and freshness into a country-style interior.

The natural vegetable dye woad can give a piercing cool blue shade when used to dye fabrics or added to limewash, especially when the woad is produced on cool

days with little sunshine, as the ambient temperature affects the final color. Woad is a durable and versatile blue pigment that can be traced back to the Stone Age. Produced from the leaves of the biennial plant *Isatis tinctoria*, which is native to southern Europe, woad has long been highly prized for the quality and stability of the pigment as well as for its decorative qualities. Known as "*bleu de roi,*"or "king's blue," in Renaissance Europe and used widely as a fabric dye and paint pigment during the 17th century, woad makes a highly durable paint for wood when combined with oil and turpentine. When mixed with limewash it creates a translucent and insect-repellent colorwash for wooden or plaster surfaces.

The main blue in the Shaker color palette was a light cool blue. The Shakers used natural plant dyes and clays to make their paints and dye their fabrics. To suit a Shaker environment the paint should be matte rather than gloss and, for real authenticity, casein or milk paint; some of them are still being made from the original recipes.

Fresh and energizing, blue marries well with a host of other colors, a quality that makes it an ideal choice for decorating a country interior. The traditional pairing of blue and white has a familiar homespun feel and has a rich

and enduring appeal for those seeking a country-style interior. It remains popular for everyday kitchen crockery, calico curtains, and bed coverings in a variety of checkered patterns, delicate spotted designs, or bold textured stripes that can be layered and mixed in countless combinations.

The fashion for blue-and-white decoration looks back for inspiration to the 17th century and the arrival of vast quantities of Chinese porcelain on European shores. Norway exported a large amount of cobalt pigment to China in the 18th and 19th centuries. The cross-pollination of ideas led to cool blue chinoiserie decoration which can be evidenced in many of the houses in the Glomdal Museum in Elverum, Norway. Other examples of blue-and-white decorating traditions in the country style are Delft tiles and Portuguese *azulejos*. While no longer an exotic taste, blue and white together nonetheless remain enormously appealing and uplifting.

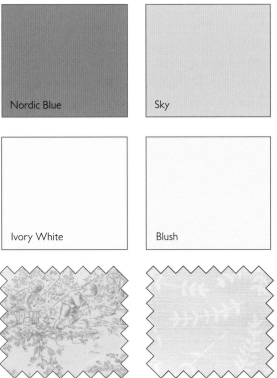

Nordic Blue	Sky
Ivory White	Blush

COLOR PALETTE Cool blue is successfully accented with pale pink. This paint color combination works well accented with toile de Jouy fabrics and simple bleached cotton or linen decorated with small sprig patterns.

Top In this bathroom in an 18th-century country house in France, the pale blue-gray tones of the woodwork are warmed by a pale yellow colorwash below dado and off-white above.

Above and right Gustavian style in Sweden in the final 20 years of the 18th century was known for its sophisticated use of the cool palette. The use of shades of blue and gray to create trompe l'oeil panels are accentuated by the use of the thin pink line edged in red. Whereas in France the side chair would have been gilded, in Scandinavia these neo-classical chairs were painted off-white.

Opposite This original 18th-century pine door is painted with a traditional blue pigment typical of homes in central France. Pine was considered an inferior wood and was always either painted or wood-grained. The door is backed by 19th-century toile de Jouy.

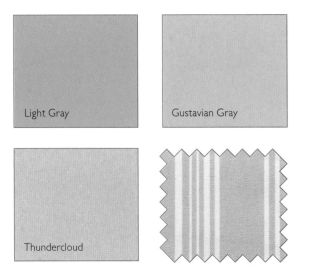

Light Gray

Gustavian Gray

Thundercloud

COLOR PALETTE Grays are soothing tones that stand up especially well to dominant fabric accessories, such as strong, wide color bands, thinner stripes, or graphic checks.

Left The palette of the icy, pale gray-green kitchen cabinets has been chosen to reflect the colors of the isolated Hardangervidda mountain plateau in Norway.

Cool and elegant, gray is perfect for making a subtly nuanced statement. From deep, near-black slate to pewter and pale dove, all shades and tones have a place.

grays

Gray and its neighbor black are very much at home in a country-style house interior. Although it may seem at odds with the country aesthetic, the color gray offers up an exciting and provocative dimension to the cool color scheme. The hard and durable natural stones of the earth—slate, granite, fieldstone, flint, and zinc, among others—bring not only color, but also texture into the country-style interior. The subtle gray-to-black shades of rough-hewn local stone celebrate the landscape, whether they are lining the walls of a bedroom, a living room, or bath. Used in the sumptuously carved stone framing a fireplace surround, fieldstones bring the outside into an interior inspired by a taste for the country.

Apart from its natural origins, gray has a venerable artistic heritage. Paynes' Gray, named for the 18th-century English watercolorist William Payne, is a less intense shade

Left In a Tuscan kitchen the off-white walls are offset by light gray cabinetry and metal stools and accented by the pale blue painted woodwork on the window surround and shutters.

Opposite From the rough gray plaster of the walls to the shades of gray and black fabrics, this country kitchen in the French home of Ebba Lopez is comfortable while elegant.

of black, achieved by mixing differing amounts of ultramarine with black. Davy's gray, a steel-like shade resulting from a combination of powdered slate, iron oxide, and carbon, was the creation of 19th-century painter Henry Davy. These artists' colors can also provide the inspiration for interior color schemes.

Decorating the rooms of a country dwelling with paints in dark, delicious tones—ranging from deep inky black to subtle shades of charcoal and the murky and cloudy grays of lead, ash, mist, and fog—add depth and contrast to a cool color scheme. The central idea behind the country-style philosophy is one of warmth and comfort. Like the jewel-like ruby, sapphire and emerald color palette, the black of onyx and caviar also succeeds in giving the rooms of a country-style dwelling a cozy, albeit rich, ambience. In the 19th-century industrial cities and coalmining centers such as Sheffield, England and Pittsburgh, Pennsylvania, the polluted environment and the extensive use of firelight and candlelight made interiors darken naturally to a deep nuanced gray.

Adding a white or cream-colored pigment to black in varying degrees will result in the delicious spectrum of gray shades—pale and cool or deep, gloomy, and rich. What makes black and gray at home in the cool range of

Silver Streak

Steel

Cashmere

Heath

COLOR PALETTE There are many tones of gray and they tend to work well together. They are ideally accented by white and off-white and can be made quite feminine when paired with lace, textured cottons and antique or modern floral *boutis*, or quilt.

colors is the ability to marry beautifully with other colors while adding a graphic edge—from light blue to pale lavender and lush purple, from celery green to the sumptuous fir green of the forest, from crimson, vermilion, and burgundy to cocoa brown, buff, and tan, and on to primrose yellow and gold.

Glossy or matte, the color black stands out as one of the most striking and sophisticated accents for an interior dedicated to the country. Whether used to trim a door, a mirror, or a window frame, to punctuate the baluster of a staircase, the paneling of a dining room, the baseboard of a bedroom, or the tiles paving a kitchen or a conservatory that is filled with a host of luscious green plants, black proves the ideal match. Black is also the perfect foil for pastel as well as bright colors, such as pink and white window curtains in stripes or checkerboard patterns, the rich scarlet of a Persian carpet, or the soft blue green of ceramic tiles lining the floor of a bath.

Gray and black are natural partners. Used together for furnishing textiles, bed quilts and coverlets, drapes and pillows, scatter rugs, window curtains, and kitchen embellishments such as pleated fabric skirts used to conceal unsightly pots and pans, they are both durable and beautiful. The combination also enhances architectural features, including black cabinet doors married with bleached gray wall paneling, the deep dark charcoal of ceiling beams reflected in the faded ash hues of clay tiled floors, a black kitchen stove set against a pale granite-colored wall, inky floorboards that show a fire surround made of local fieldstone. This pairing brings a sophisticated flavour to a country-style interior.

Gray is a color that occurs in both traditional and modern country interiors. In a seaside cottage on Nantucket located in the icy Atlantic waters, crisp whites, cool creams, and pale grays reflect the frosty climate of the surrounding countryside. In a modern country house, older and more colorful country elements often mix with the gray of polished aluminum kitchen appliances, glass-topped dining tables, Eames-style chairs, and brushed-steel lighting fixtures, finding a balance between traditional and modern.

Left, above The shade of matte gray on this paneled wall was chosen by Jeffery Bilhuber from the tones in the Connecticut fieldstone originally used to build this Federal home in 1827.

Left, center The rough plaster walls of this Upstate New York 1800s farmhouse are painted oyster white with a frieze in shades of gray. The 1940s kitchen cabinets are sprayed chrome. Some of the surfaces are painted silver.

Left, below In this quintessentially feminine bedroom in Connecticut, the late 19th-century iron bed is draped with brilliant white lace. The walls are covered with a pale gray faux-shagreen wallpaper.

Opposite The solid gray walls in this Normandy bedroom form a stark contrast to the plasterwork and artwork. The color is reflected in the metal copy of a 19th-century bed frame. The color accent is achieved with the 19th-century floral French *boutis*.

COLOR PALETTE Grays, while essentially muted and masculine, can be given a dramatic twist with strong accent colors, such as terra-cotta or vermilion.

Lead

Crimson

A symbol of nobility and experience in Japanese culture and associated with the life-giving soil for Native Americans, the color black proves to be a cooling accent to a host of earth-born shades—for the moldings surrounding the paneling of walls painted in pale terra-cotta hues, for baseboards and door frames, for the trimming of a woollen blanket colored in a riotous plaid of sharp crimson, citrus yellow, and pistachio green. It is a distinctive shade for the furniture that decorates a country interior, whether used for a dining table painted in rich ebony, a wooden mirror frame, a leather chair, or the deep satiny finish of a cast iron bed frame. Black is most sophisticated when paired with natural shades such as driftwood, stone, and bark in cool and clean modern interiors, and also shows off to great advantage the golden glowing hues of pine, walnut, and light fruitwoods.

Above and Right Gray, black, and stark white bathroom fixtures create a calm, cool, and highly practical environment. Natural deep gray slate is used for the basin and the backsplash of the bathtub.

Opposite Country-style color can be inspired by the simplest of choices. Designer Dominique Kieffer took the scheme in this Normandy farmhouse hallway of grays, off-whites, and blacks from the original simple marble flooring. The gray doorway frames the entrance to the deep red room beyond.

warm colors

THE INFORMAL AMBIENCE of the Mediterranean interior is shaped by the sumptuous colors and abundant patterns found in the rich fertile landscape. From the dusty reds and deep browns of the sun-baked deserts of Morocco and Santa Fe, to the rolling, beige-and-green vine-clad hills of Tuscany and Umbria, and across the vibrant sunny yellow valleys of southern France, colors for decorating the interiors of country dwellings traditionally have been borrowed from the countryside. The palette comprised of the warm pinks, terra-cottas, and golden yellows of the earth has been the source of comfort and solace in the decoration of country interiors, a delicious foil for the cooling greens and blues of local flowers, fruits, and herbs.

The stone or clay-built farmhouse, or *mas*, of Provence echoes the robust combinations of brilliant hues—burnt oranges, bitter lemons, cobalt blues, and sunflower yellows—of the surrounding farmland. Beneath a bright sapphire sky, red terra-cotta roof tiles glisten in the golden sun. The deep russet earth of the rugged, red clay hills dotted with olive and chestnut trees provides a warm and intense background for lush green foliage, fields of lavender, sunflowers, and red poppies that stretch into the distance. These colors are brought into the interior in a variety of ways, in colorful cotton furnishing fabrics patterned with fruit, flowers, or simple geometric designs on backgrounds of buff, mustard, or cherry red; in glossy ceramic tiles in shades of lime green, crimson, and citrus yellow that border a fireplace surround; or a kitchen floor laid with local stone or brick reflecting the rich warm reds of the local earth.

By contrast, the stone country dwelling in Italy reflects the faded pinks, buffs, and soft warm golden ochers of the Tuscan hills. Inside, roughly plastered walls generously borrow the palette of the landscape for decoration—weather-beaten shades of burnt sienna, dry earthy tones of terra-cotta and ocher that absorb the daytime heat, along with cooler tints taken from the herbs that grow in hazy drifts across the sun-baked Italian countryside, including the green of thyme and the warm tones of lavender. Soft, mellow wooden chairs, hutches, and tables, furnishing fabrics and tiles in bold combinations of yellow and blue or red with green add a lively note to the pinks, buffs, terra-cottas, and ochers used on the colorwashed walls.

Opposite, from top The colors of the earth and the interesting mix of pattern and texture bring a Moroccan feel to this Tuscan farmhouse.

The use of brick red on some of the walls adds warmth to a Connecticut living area.

The original 1750s wide plank walls are painted in a traditional Colonial color. In some houses of this period ox blood was used to stain the boards. It is the perfect backdrop for an 18th-century American ladder-back rocker.

This vaulted ceiling dominates the warm natural pigment on the walls of this Tuscan farmhouse.

The yellow colorwash on the walls of this bathroom is given added impact by the blue and brown painted paneling.

In this Germantown, New York, house from the 1870s the bright yellow walls contrast with the classical white painted fire-surround and white fabrics.

Opposite The use of rectangular blocks of warm beige, bordered in white, gives a modern twist to the paneled Tuscan bedroom designed by Ilaria Miani. The modern iron bed frame is inspired by 19th-century French bed designs.

Right In a French country house the warm soft ocher tones of the colorwash are further warmed by traditional floral French quilts, or *boutis*, and faded Persian rugs.

Toffee Cream

Cord

COLOR PALETTE These pale, warm earth tones complement off-whites and neutrals. They work particularly well with simple textured fabrics with small prints, checks, and stripes.

The warm, comforting tones of yellow have a long and satisfying pedigree in the decoration of country homes the world over. The earth has offered up sun-drenched hues and rich pigments that create an uplifting ambiance.

yellow earth tones

The sumptuous golden colors of the earth bring a satisfying sense of wellbeing and contentment into the rooms of a country dwelling. Uplifting, warm yellows are found in the luminous color of a sun-drenched field of ripening grain, sunflowers, or harvest vegetables including acorn, butternut squash, and pumpkins. The yellows of the earth create a spicy saturated palette of saffron, mustard, and chutney and the mellow, muted ocher and umber, burnt sienna, and burnt orange hues derived from the clay and sand of the landscape. These earthy colours are favored for the mottled

colorwashed walls of a farmhouse nestled on an Italian hillside, an adobe house in Santa Fe, or a simple Gujarati mud hut in India. The spectrum of earth yellows is at once hospitable and cheerful, softening the light and providing a glowing backdrop for a host of furnishing colors, from indigo blue to deep fir, lime green, charcoal, inky black or shocking combinations of hot pink, vermilion, or ruby red.

Perhaps nowhere are the warm yellow colors of the earth more at home than in Italy's provinces of Tuscany and Umbria. The brickwork, stucco, and tiles of houses perched

Above In the inner courtyard of a traditionally designed house near Santa Fe, the warmth of the brick floor, the natural earth plasters, and the pine ceiling beams mirror the high desert environment.

Right The plaster walls of this Santa Fe house, designed by Baker-Laporte, have been finished with earth pigments. The warmth of the pine corbel screen and circular roof beams is echoed in the Arizona flagstone floor and fireplace.

Below, right Raw plaster, tinted with native pigment before application, lines the walls in this Santa Fe home. The walls are then polished with beeswax to give a subtle sheen.

Opposite The soft pale yellow colorwash in this Virginian bedroom, designed by Solis Betancourt, is further enhanced with natural linens, quilts, and 18th-century furniture.

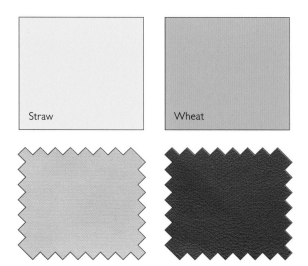

Straw	Wheat

COLOR PALETTE From natural adobe in New Mexico to pale yellow colorwash in Virginia, earth tones work best with natural fabrics; from sheer cottons to leather.

high in hilltop villages, or nestled among the olive and lemon groves, bask in the warm and golden tones of Italian light, which celebrate the sun-bleached pinks and golden ochers derived from local soils and clay. The interiors boast thick naturally worn rough-plastered walls awash with the earthy muted yellow shades that lie at the heart of the Tuscan palette, umber, yellow-ocher, and burnt sienna, which have been applied in water-based matte washes that create subtle gradations of color across the wall surfaces rather than solid blocks of saturated color.

These same hues are mirrored in vibrant furnishing textiles—which are often punctuated with accents in terra-cotta, copper reddish pinks, and reds—and in the polished natural wood tones (especially walnut and chestnut) of tables, chairs, and hutches. The most popular cooler hues to temper the warm colors (apart from the ubiquitous white favored for ceilings) are the medley of blue and green shades found in plants native to Tuscany, such as thyme, and the grayish tones of olive green, lilac, and lavender blue.

Across the globe from Africa to Northern Europe earth yellows, which originate from ocher and raw

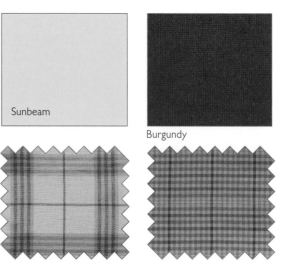

Sunbeam

Burgundy

COLOR PALETTE Good strong yellow tones are nicely accented by plum and black. The cotton fabrics used have earth tones of terra-cotta, cream, and beige in stripes and checks.

sienna, have enjoyed a long history of widespread use for the decoration of country-style interiors. As with other pigments derived from the earth, these yellows, while never quite matching the radiance of a true primary color, can be incredibly vivid and bright. Yellow reflects the quality of light surrounding it. In soft morning light, yelows take on a gentle glow, while in bright mid-day sun yellow will be vibrant and lively. At once invigorating, and warm, as well as sophisticated and mood-enhancing, earth yellows have a long tradition for wall finishes, creating a soft and mellifluous light that enhances a variety of color combinations—navy blue and white, hot pink and leaf green, daffodil yellow and ruby red, turquoise and coral—for window curtains, tablecloths, bed coverings, hooked rugs, and kitchen crockery.

In the sun-drenched landscape of countries including Morocco, Egypt, and Tunisia, the sands, clays, and soils are the source of many of the construction materials and pigments used in local houses. Inspiration for the warm North African earth colored palette is comprised of a heady spectrum of sumptuous yellows, including mustard, gold, ocher, and umber with accents of pinks and pinkish reds. The traditional application of *tadelakt*, a

Above The walls in the sitting room of this Tuscan farmhouse designed by Ilaria Miani are painted a specially mixed yellow with plum baseboards. The colors reflect the local wildflowers found in the Orcia Valley in the spring.

Right In the kitchen the same wall color is finished off with black baseboards. These colors are picked up in the specially designed table, lights, and log container.

Opposite The simplicity of the design is deceptive: the traditional wooden ceiling structure and brick floor are given a modern twist by the color choice and large, simple, black painted window frame.

Sunshine

Sunflower

French Gray

COLOR PALETTE The warm tones of yellow, whether applied as a colorwash or solid color, have been popular for centuries. Accents of white or gray tone down the brightness and support interesting fabrics, from stripes to modern equivalents of Elizabethan flame stitch.

compound of sand, quicklime, and earth-colored pigments, to the interior walls of Moroccan dwellings produces a lustrous finish ranging from dark brown to rich red, or from pinkish red to pale tobacco, depending on which pigments and types of sand are used.

To tone down these warm shades of the earth, cooling whites, light sands, and soil colors such as pale gold, sandstone, and beige are used, especially for wall finishes. An extensive vocabulary of greens—inspired by the colors of Moroccan orchards and gardens and a color symbolic of Islam—offers refuge from the sizzling sun. Also complementary are a variety of blue tones, pinks, strong reds, and purples used for decorative wall and floor tiles, painted furniture, brightly colored carpets and furnishing textiles, and structural features such as louvered screens, wooden doors, and window frames.

The sunny, intense yellows of sunflowers and lemons, the bright vibrant umbers, burnt siennas, and ochers, pale champagne golds, and flaxen shades are well-suited to the decoration of a country-style interior. Yellow can be successfully incorporated into the country house in a variety of ways, fabrics include window curtains, bed coverlets, pillows, and the upholstery of chairs and sofas;

Above The color scheme of the main reception room in a house in Columbia County, New York, was popular when the house was modernized in the Greek Revival style in the 1840s. The two-tone yellow reflected the importance of the room.

Left The pale yellow-ocher distemper colorwash on the walls, the brickwork of the vaulted ceiling and the faded terra-cotta floor tiles of the entrance hall provide a seamless passage from the outside in. The pale blue of the plank door complements these earthy tones.

Left, below Interiors in 19th-century homes in Upstate New York were often painted in tones of yellow and red with white painted woodwork. The white painted Queen Anne-style chairs are a modern twist.

Opposite In Tuscany earth pigments can vary from intense yellows and reds to muted terra-cotta, often with hints of brown. The dining room walls are painted with a yellow-brown distemper colorwash.

Left Two-toned stripes are used in this bedroom in Tuscany. The addition of white mutes the yellow umber.

Above and Opposite In a Perigord *chartreuse* many tones of yellow have been used throughout the house, including this bedroom and en-suite bathroom. In these north-facing rooms strong, intense yellows, rather than pale shades, are used to good effect.

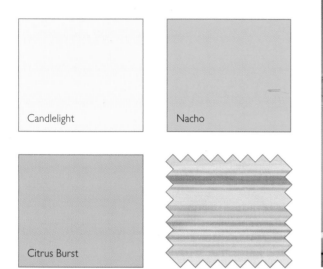

Candlelight

Nacho

Citrus Burst

COLOR PALETTE Yellow, particularly with ocher added, can make as strong a statement as red. This is accentuated when other bright colors are used in striped fabrics.

walls can be softly colorwashed in pale ocher or umber, brightly painted in the color of buttercups, or papered with an array of designs in sunshine hues; floor treatments include local mellow brick, bright glossy tile, or carpets and scatter rugs; even kitchen accessories can add a dash of warm yellow in earthenware plates, cups and saucers, and serving platters. Earth yellows work well in concert with the verdant greens of vegetables—peas, pale celery, cucumbers, and beans—the bright indigo blue of cornflowers, the pale violet blues of lavender and lilacs, the deep blushing pinks of roses, or the pale pink whisper of primroses. Pale gold in a bright array of checkerboards and stripes, bold flower patterns, or the random scattering of delicate blossoms are given a sharp modern edge when punctuated with inky black or the charcoal grays found in the natural slate, fieldstone, and granite of the landscape.

These are but a few of the ways that earth yellows colors bring life into the bedrooms, living rooms, kitchens, and terraces of a country dwelling.

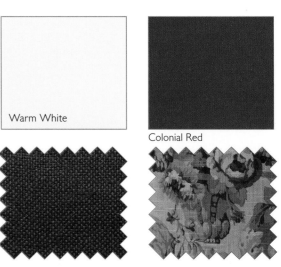

COLOR PALETTE There is nothing that evokes a sense of the Colonial period better than a historical red matched with natural linens and a faded floral fabric.

Warm White

Colonial Red

Of all the colors born from the natural landscape, it is the rich, ripe red pigments of the earth that bring a warm personality and piquant flavor to the country-house interior.

red earth tones

Above and Opposite The inner sanctum of this 1754 house in Litchfield, Connecticut, by Champalimaud Design, is the Keeping or Long Room. The paneling above the inglenook fireplace and under the dado rail is painted Colonial Red. This is off-set above dado by an off-white. The colors in the room are enhanced by the Persian carpet of traditional design. These carpets, known as Turkey rugs, were highly prized.

The colors and decorative traditions that can be found in hot and sunny climates—ranging from a farmhouse in the south of France to a hacienda in Santa Fe and from a colorful villa in Marrakesh to a stucco cottage nestled in the Italian hillside village of Montalcino—have for generations looked for inspiration to the reds of the surrounding landscape. Rich, vibrant, and warm, the delicious and dazzling variegated shades of terra-cotta, crimson, and pink are punctuated by the flowers and foliage of the native terrain. Accents to the reds come from the spectrum of verdant greens found in herbs such as sage and thyme, in grapevines, and in olive and lemon groves. Blues accents include violet, lavender, and peacock. The distinctive colors of native birds, plants and flowers, fruits and

vegetables, and soils and clays, ultimately find their way into the country-house interior.

The robust, spicy family of scarlet earth colors—terra-cottas, warm oranges, vermilion, pinkish reds, and deep earth crimsons—complements the natural palette of golden wood tones, neutral whites and creams, beiges, pale ashes, slates, and stone grays. The band of terra-cotta colors also embraces the luscious hues of autumn, ranging from a crisp and sharp burnt orange to scarlet red and the deep violet of eggplant. The bold intense earth colors found on sun-ripened fruit, such as russet-red apples, crimson pears, the purple of plums, grapes and radicchio, the blood-red of beetroot and pomegranates and the coral and blush orange of peaches, are but a few of the dazzling color inspirations that originate

100

COLOR PALETTE Using different tones of pinks and reds in a room adds to the visual stimulation. It can be a subtle tonal variation, but it adds texture to the color palette.

Rich Red

Rouge

Rose

Battleship

Opposite Good use of pink and terra-cotta pigments cleverly lead the eye from the arch of this Tuscan farmhouse to the window at the end of the corridor. The off-white walls are banded by a black stripe that mirrors the black painted baseboard.

Left Deep reds with black woodwork can be softened by the use of white upholstery and cushions, as demonstrated so well in the salon of this Normandy manor house.

Below Red earth tones are used to accentuate the architecture in this 18th-century Tuscan conversion. The colors subtly change from pale pink to deeper red to a warm orange umber. The contrasting architrave is painted pale gray.

from the earth. A number of spicy colors that make up the rich, sun-lit palette that is typical of the sumptuous textiles of India—deep reds and pinks, glittering golds, pink-golds, and nutmeg browns—touch the imagination and make up yet another seminal component of the terra-cotta spectrum.

These time-honored colors have been used both inside and outside of country-style dwellings throughout the world—from the soft, mellow shades covering the walls of a villa nestled in the Tuscan hills to the bold sun-drenched hues found on the terrace tiles of a Provençal farmhouse. Some of these shades at times can be quite vivid and bright, depending upon the surrounding light. But others can be soft and warm and easy to live with and are ideal for the walls or floors of a sitting room or bedroom.

The rich palette of terra-cotta colors creates a handsome backdrop for furniture and textiles, either as paint or colorwash covering the walls and reflecting light or as curtains hung at the windows allowing light to filter softly through. The glow reflected from warm terra-cotta, literally "fired earth," shows furniture, paintings, textiles, and decorative artifacts to best advantage. The light in these rooms at any time of the day projects a radiant luminosity that suggests the evening sunset of the Mediterranean.

In the interior, terra-cotta comes into its own naturally in the form of tiled floors and plastered walls. At the

lighter end of the spectrum terra-cotta takes shape in the appealing rustic hue of raw plaster reminiscent of a rough sun-baked surface, delightfully uneven, warm, and very compatible with the soft mellow patina of timeworn polished wood. These colors also call to mind the Pompeiian red which so captivated the architects and designers of the 18th-century Neoclassical period and which still has a place in contemporary country style. Darker incarnations of terra-cotta lean toward a deep red-brown and marry especially well with the refreshing contrast of white combined with blue or black, for example, checked or striped textile fabrics, blue and white kitchen crockery, or black and white tiled floors.

These saturated, hot earth tones are cooled when partnered with a palette consisting of frosty and creamy

whites and the pale colors of the soil, such as biscuit, beige, stone, sand, and faded gold. Vegetative shades also offer calm contrast with warm reds and relief from sizzling temperatures. Textiles—window curtains, bed coverlets, scatter rugs, soft coverings, and upholstery—in a dazzling spectrum of greens resonate with the colors of a Colonial New England herb garden including thyme, sage, mint, and rosemary, or of the olive groves and vines indigenous to the Tuscan hills or the luscious pine forests, cacti, and shading palms native to the Mexican desert.

Below The warm colors of the walls in this living room in Tuscany contrast with the cold gray of the late 19th-century fire surround and fireplace wall. The colors in the late 19th-century tiles in the fire surround are picked up in the fabrics.

Opposite Although the colors and patterns of this room in a Tuscan farmhouse may give the impression of North Africa, they are also associated with the Italian Renaissance. This is particularly true of the gilded detail. The deep terra-cotta of the vaulted ceiling focuses attention on the patterned wall below. The 19th-century double closet fits seamlessly into the decorative scheme.

Other ways of bringing a refreshing cool and calm ambience into the interior of a country dwelling surrounded by the sun-burnt colors typical of a hot, parched climate include combining the pale reds, golds, and greens found in apple, pear, and peach orchards with the soft blues of lavender that stretch across the fields of Norfolk in England; the lilacs and wistaria hovering above a pergola that takes pride of place in the ample back garden of a southern plantation-style dwelling in North Carolina, Virginia, and Tennessee; or even the intense royal blues of the abundant cornflowers that grow across fields from California to Austria.

Whether painted on the walls to reflect light, or hung at windows for light to filter softly through, warm terra-cotta colors bring forth a background that is both flattering and alluring, and very much a country look.

Tomato

Pepper

Tuscan Olive

Marlin

COLOR PALETTE A warm, patterned wall or textile can often be best accented with pale linens that pick up the background tones.

Blues with any hint of red in them fall into the warm camp. These are the colors found in hotter locations, with an intensity and depth to match the climate.

warm blues

Warm blues are the colors of the Mediterranean, of the southern states of America, of Mexico and of North Africa, those places where the sun is strong and the natural pigments are much denser, in order to withstand this blazing intensity. Warm blues can be found in the luminous color of the sea lapping the shores of the Cote d'Azur and in the purity of the cloudless sapphire skies blazing with sizzling yellow sunshine on Provençal fields, or flooding a Moroccan courtyard with light. Spacious and breezy, blue lifts the spirits and creates an unmatched feeling of wellbeing. Warm-toned blues range from violet to powder blue, from French navy to the lustrous blues found in flowers such as delphiniums and

Summer Sky

Lapis

Soft Violet

COLOR PALETTE Saturated blues can be warm colors, especially when they are associated with mauves and lilacs. Exotic striped fabrics, in cotton or silk, with tones of pink and red, accentuate the warmth.

Left In this Tuscan farmhouse in the hills above Lucca, the bathroom is painted in tones of lavender with special breathable paints, suitable for use in a steamy bathroom. All the colors reflect the countryside.

Opposite Again the lavender walls and blue-green shutters reflect the Tuscan hills. The blue, green, terra-cotta, and lavender beds are painted with milk paint. The fine cotton drapes add a touch of North African style.

Above, left and center In these Moroccan homes the distinctive vibrant blue pigment is often combined with green—the colors of the peacock brought together. This blue has a great deal of red in it and is at once soothing and energizing.

Above right These 19th-century table and chairs have been painted in sky and royal blue. Country furniture makers often used cheap woods that were intended to be painted. This was both a practical approach and aesthetically pleasing. The addition of simple red and white cushions adds to the informality.

Opposite Bright blue shutters can be found all over southern France. They were originally painted with the vegetable pigment woad, which was a natural insect repellent. They blend with the natural stone of this farmhouse designed by Kathryn Ireland, not far from Toulouse, known as "La Ville Rose" because of the delicate purplish-pink of the stone.

bluebells. Indigo, an organic vegetable dye, is the source of nature's purest and warmest blue and for centuries was the sole affordable version of the color. The intense blue found in the highly prized mineral lapis lazuli was too costly for use in the interior. Indigo blue, which fades over time, is at its most elegant on architectural features such as careworn blue-gray paneling or pale washed-out quilts. Other blue shades include azurite, ultramarine, and cerulean blue. The palette was broadened considerably by the invention of Prussian blue in the early 18th century and synthetic blues in the 19th century.

With its undertones of red, lavender is the freshest, and most countrified of the blue palette. A soft, quiet color, lavender becomes lively when married with its natural partner white, or used with accents of yellow and green. This combination of colors is most frequently observed decorating the exteriors of houses in hot climates ranging from Morroco to Greece, where they reflect the harsh white light with dazzling intensity.

A more electric partnership of dazzling richness lies in the contrast of the opposites blue and yellow, which finds inspiration in the colors of nature, such as the yellow

center of a blue flower or the sun in the summer sky. In strong light this vibrant, inspired combination—sky blue accented with lemon, duck egg blue with pale wheat highlights, light blue set off by primrose, or powder blue trimmed with sunshine yellow—for curtains, upholstery, or wall paneling, enlivens a room. The pairing of blue and yellow is most successful when the tones of the two shades are complementary, whether offset against each other as blocks of dense color, matched within an identical floral print, or used in different proportions with one color furnishing a sharp accent trimming for a fabric, architectural molding, window frame, or cabinet doors. Green is the result when blue and yellow are mixed and the fundamental harmony and balance of this hue is suggested in decorative blue and yellow color schemes.

Blue and green—where the lush green hills of the landscape join the cloudy pale turquoise of the sea—is a familiar and natural color partnership. Hues from violet to blue and from aquamarine to green mingle easily. The sharp edgy relationship between the two colors has traditionally evoked a sense of excitement and magic, especially in the assortment of blue greens, from seagreen

Blue Lagoon

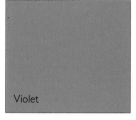

Violet

Brazilian

Island Green

COLOR PALETTE In hot climates, from Morocco to Provence, the use of a variety of blue tones reflects the intense blue of the sky. Fabrics such as striped silks, cottons with Provençal prints, and brightly colored checks are all appropriate.

109

and jade to turquoise, a hue that was highly prized in Tibet as well as by the Egyptians, Incas, and Persians. The pale blue green known as "apothecary blue" was favored for decoration of interiors in Federal America. Forming a visual and olfactory connection with the surrounding countryside are the blues and greens found in the verdant native plants of Tuscany—sage and euphorbias, for example—that transform an Italian villa into a cool and refreshing refuge from the sizzling hot climate.

Eye-catching and spirited, yet at the same time soothing and calm, aquamarine, found where the blue of the sea meets the green of the sea floor, is a shade that is frequently found lavishly splashed throughout the interiors of houses located in countries where the light is bright and strong, such as Morocco or Tunisia. Never neutral, this blue is stimulating, but not tiring on the eye, and is a challenging color for the bedroom or living room. It is a hue that has given inspiration to a number of 20th-century artists, including Henri Matisse and Paul Klee.

Blue is ideal for the bed covers, scatter pillows, drapes, and carpets that decorate a country-style bedroom, to create a warm and welcoming refuge from the stresses of everyday life. For the tiles and towels dotted around a bathroom, look to lavender blues for inspiration. Whether used to paint shutters or doors, as a backdrop covering the walls of a kitchen, or given voice as an accent shade, the halcyon warm blues symbolize comfort and relaxation, qualities that lie at the heart of country style.

Island Blue

Lake Blue

COLOR PALETTE Warm blues are often associated with off-white. This color scheme works well with either warm off-white striped or check cottons. Chinese carpets, with their distinctive blue "dragon chasing the pearl of wisdom" design, are another successful addition.

Left In this 18th-century Connecticut home the paneling and doors are painted in a warm blue colorwash. The distressed look replicates how the original paint would have been applied. The owners have researched the original colors in the rooms by painstakingly scraping back the paint layers to reveal the colors from different periods.

Opposite In a bedroom the bright blue outline of the shutters and woodwork against the off-white walls creates a sunny feel, reminiscent as it is of summer skies with clouds.

Below In an Indian dining area sky blue is accented with green and yellow. The curtains, inspired by traditional saris, are light and airy—diffusing the light rather than eliminating it.

hot colors

STRONG VIBRANT COLORS are very much at home in a country-house setting. At first glance rich crimsons, bright pinks, electric blues, and saturated greens might appear at odds with a country aesthetic that has been founded on the principles of comfort and relaxation. But it is the sheer dynamism of these hues that breathes life into a country interior while offering up the perfect foil for the display of simple everyday objects. These colors lift the spirit and enhance a room with a healthy dose of confidence and imagination.

The palette of hot tones that inspired country interiors crops up across the world, from the vivid scarlets and vermilions, intense yellows, purples, and magentas of tulips in the flower fields of Holland to the exuberant blues and greens of the shores of a sun-drenched Caribbean island. The joy of decorating with rich scorching colors is not confined to a sophisticated apartment in the heart of Paris or a grand country house in Santa Fe. Bright colors in all their glorious shades also bring life to a small dwelling nestled in a modest Palm Beach neighborhood. Fearless combinations of bright colors that complement each other in fresh ways result in an interior that is adventurous, dramatic, and highly original.

Hot saturated colors furnish the ideal backdrop for engaging patterns of both functional objects and decorative items. A wall painted in the fiery vermilion, vivid green, or bright yellow typically found in the riotous patterns of cotton fabrics from Africa shows off to good advantage a kitchen cabinet lined with colorful kitchen crockery and glassware, a bookshelf heaving with rows of books, or a mahogany corner cupboard sheltering a treasured collection of sculpture and ceramics. Hot pink, sapphire blue, or emerald cleverly set off with equal panache a single primitive painting, an overmantel mirrorglass, a tile fire surround, a pair of glossy Chinese porcelain vases, a bronze bust, or humble decorative items, such as wooden boxes, woven baskets, or wall lights made of pewter or brass. Vivid reds, dazzling blues, moody greens, and glorious yellows can be juxtaposed in endless and often boisterous combinations that are tempered by the pale dry shades—light terra-cottas, buffs, and soft yellows—that reflect the warm dust of an arid sand-colored desert in the hot sultry climates and the scorched earth of Africa and India.

Opposite, from top This vibrant solid blue wall provides the perfect canvas for brightly colored flowers.

In a home in Mexico City, the walls of the dining room are a distinctive and dramatic mottled orange red.

In Mexico, wherever you travel you are constantly aware of the ubiquitous "rosa Mexicana," or Mexican pink.

Again in Mexico this vibrant purple works with the rosa Mexicana. The famous Mexican architect Luis Barragan wrote "Color is a complement to architecture. It can be used to widen or enclose a space. It is also imperative for adding that touch of magic to an area."

In India the choice of color is like selecting a jewel. The color of the room has to delight the senses to be successful.

Deep solid red on the walls is contrasted with the check cotton sheer curtain for a vibrant statement.

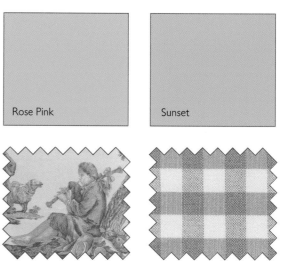

Rose Pink Sunset

COLOR PALETTE A bright pink is used in a cool country to brighten the senses. This feminine scheme is continued with the fabrics, a small check gingham and an ever-popular toile de Jouy.

If you are looking for inspiration for a vibrant color scheme, what better place to start than the garden and forest? Nature knows best when it comes to putting together powerful combinations and shimmering shades.

flower power

Above Flowers, the inspiration for this 18th-century Dutch house's decorative scheme by Floriene Bosch, is one of the most resonant of country themes. In the dining room, the pink of the walls is echoed in the toile de Jouy tablecloth. The white painted 19th-century French dining chairs are covered in two tones of spring green. The English 19th-century Staffordshire plates made for the Dutch market feature windmills.

Opposite Again in the living room the jewel-like effect is created by the solid pink walls, fabrics, and drapes contrasting with the gloss white of the woodwork and fire surround.

When contemplating the colors of the country, it is the indigenous flowers, trees, and plants that immediately spring to mind. These are the colors of the landscape that play a key role in the decoration of a country-style interior. From the tulips stretching across the fields and parks of Holland to the lilacs and lavenders surrounding the villas of the American South, flowers for centuries have informed the decoration of living rooms, kitchens, bedrooms, baths, and verandas. Flowers delight, refresh, and are pleasing to the eye. Their palettes, uniquely borne from nature, both stimulate and inspire.

Fruit and flowers and their colors are at heart feminine, delicate, and gentle on the eye. From the strong, vibrant primary palette—red, blue, and yellow—a limitless variety of heady combinations are created, such as the greens of limes and apples, grass, and fir trees; the purples of plums, lavender, and lilacs; the blues of irises and bluegrass; the oranges of tiger lilies and blood oranges. Mixed together or enhanced by the addition of white or black, primary colors for the country house cover the broad spectrum of the fruits and flowers found in nature.

It is with the addition of white—in large or small doses—that primary colors spring to life and conjure up images of tulips, roses, lilacs, lavenders, hyacinths, hydrangeas, primroses, and sweetpeas. In a host of tints the red of cherries and hot peppers were transformed into the luxurious and feminine pinks favored for the sumptuous satins, floral brocades, and

Desert Sky

Blue Sea

COLOR PALETTE Bright blues with white accents can be warmed by the use of floral fabrics, from toiles to pink-and-white and blue-and-white floral cottons.

Opposite In the guest cottage of a Dutch house, the inspiration of flowers is apparent. The plank walls are painted different shades of blue and the fabrics—toiles, hand-painted florals, and simple printed cottons—create the desired effect. The paintings give the context of the inspiration.

Right and Below Again, simple ginghams and solid pale pink chair coverings contrast with the gloss white of the woodwork and display cabinet. The owner's collections of 19th-century floral porcelains emphasize the overall theme.

striped cottons that were used to flattering effect for the wall hangings, drapes, carpets, and upholstery that decorated the private apartments of Madame de Pompadour in 18th-century France. When white is added, the bright magentas and crimsons, typical of the East and of poppies stretched across the French countryside, can be turned into the soothing pale pink of cotton candy. Sapphire blues are turned into the light powdery shades of bluebells, harebells, and the sky.

An intense shade of yellow metamorphoses into the delicate hues of goldenrod or in the pale flaxen colors of field grasses and buttercups growing throughout the hills of the south of France or the golden hues that stretch across the Sonoma Valley of California. Vibrant greens are changed to the color of freshcut grass, a local lime, or the stem of a flower.

The power of flowers cannot be underestimated in decoration. The fertile landscape brings forth variegated colors of blossoms and shrubs that, when used for a color scheme, add charm and a homespun quality to a bedroom, a kitchen, or a sitting room. These colors include the elegant colors of roses—ranging from vibrant hues of magenta to pale shades of blush pink—the soft warm yellows of daffodils or the intense vibrant golds of daisies, sunflowers, and black-eyed Susans; the rich blues and greens that echo the colors of the flowers and plants that are dotted around the sea floor; or the gray-greens of herbs such as dill, tarragon, or thyme.

The pinks, blues, and yellows found in the plants and flowers of the surrounding countryside tend to be looked upon as feminine colors that are best enjoyed and

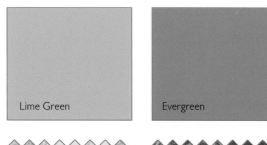

Lime Green

Evergreen

COLOR PALETTE Green is associated with the landscape, plants, and trees. In a bright palette it works best with florals, either toiles, chintz, embroidered fabrics or antique cotton quilts.

Right The fresh lime green on the plank walls resonates in the lampshades, painting, and the simple floral pattern bedspread.

Opposite The bright green painted plank wall serves as the perfect backdrop for this homage to flowers; from the simple floral chintz covered headboard to the lampshades, pillows and 19th-century French floral *boutis*, or quilt. Even the gray-painted bedside cabinets have floral swags.

Below The decorative scheme in this 18th-century Dutch salon, different tones of bright green and solid white woodwork, could have been taken from the pair of Staffordshire vases on the mantelpiece. In summer the room is bedecked with flowers.

appreciated when decorating the boudoirs, baths, and sitting rooms of young ladies in the form of wallpapers and paints, cushions and bed coverings, curtains and carpets, but all become sharp and sophisticated when married with tones such as dark emerald green, dark blue, and black. Pink remains girlie and feminine when partnered with the pale subtle shades of lettuce, celery, or pistachio nuts; with the light powder blue of the skies; with white and cream; or with the warm sunshine yellow of roses, tulips, and daffodils.

The herbs, flowers, and trees found in the lush vegetation of the local landscape inspire the decoration of a villa perched on a hilltop that overlooks the warm rich hills of Tuscany, a Moroccan hideaway surrounded by the hot, sun-baked desert, and a farmhouse nestled in the forested terrain of Maine. The colors of indigenous plants are woven into furnishing textiles, including boldly striped window curtains and upholstery for chairs and sofas, carpets and hooked rugs in checkerboard patterns, tablecloths in rich Provençal prints, and blankets and quilts for beds scattered with faded floral designs.

The term chintz has come to mean any cotton or linen floral printed furnishing fabric. This has overshadowed its true origin as carefully hand-painted fabric (calico or Indienne) from India. First exported to Europe in the early 1600s, Indian chintz textiles rapidly captivated the Western market. These were most popular in country interiors as they had the effect of bringing the garden indoors. This was, of course, especially popular in the gray days of winter.

The shades of nature are also represented in the vivid motifs of earthenware kitchen crockery and the colorwashed shades that saturate the walls of a country

Opposite In a virtual riot of color and pattern, this room rejoices with two-tone rose pink walls and ceiling bordered in white arabesque designs and carpets, cushions, and upholstery in silks, wools, and cottons—all with strong pattern.

Right Pattern is also traditional within Indian decoration and these white stylized, scrolling vegetal forms, resembling cypress, palm, and other plant forms feature prominently in Indian art. Another feature of these interiors is how one color leads into the next—a virtual feast of color.

Below This bold green room is perfectly accented by strong white. The white is used as a contrasting color but also to accentuate the architecture of the room. The color combination also follows through to the latticed white-painted chairs.

dwelling. Evoking orchards planted with fruit trees, verdant green shrubs and palms; the scent of herbs including thyme, rosemary, and sage; flower beds blooming with candy-colored yellow, pink, and violet blossoms, great color brings the outside well and tuly into the country interior.

One has only to consider the artist Vincent van Gogh's heady description of a painting of his bedroom in a letter written to his brother Theo to realize the powerful influence of the landscape and the flowers and plants that grow within it on an interior ". . . the walls are pale violet, the wood of the bed and chairs is the yellow of fresh butter, the sheet and pillows very light lemon-green. The coverlet scarlet. The window green. The toilet table range, the basin blue. The doors lilac." The sun-drenched hillsides of Provence covered with carpets of orange-red poppies or nodding sunflowers and fields of pale lavender immediately spring to mind.

Other colorful inspirations include a pergola dressed with mauve vines of wisteria; the buttery lemon yellows and delicate raspberry pinks of roses climbing over the face of a thatch-roofed cottage nestled in the Cotswolds; pots of crimson azaleas, hot-pink bougainvillea, purple pansies and yellow alamandas that bloom on the sun-drenched terrace of a Mexican hacienda; and the flower garden of a Georgian-style mansion in the heart of Savannah blooming in joyous abundance with scarlet geraniums, violets, creamy magnolias, pink tulips, and hosts of blue narcissi.

COLOR PALETTE In India bright color is treated as an essential component to the decorative scheme. Just as Shah Jahan used precious jewels to make the Taj Mahal sparkle, so color is used to radiate in an interior, especially when used with bright silks, saturated florals, and fabrics with strong contrasting patterns.

Viper Green

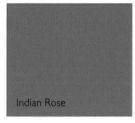

Indian Rose

Bold Orange

Above These walls in a country house in the Palmeraie of Marrakesh are covered in the traditional *tadelakt*, pigmented in a tobacco color. *Tadelakt* is a mixture of sand, quicklime, and earth-colored pigments smoothed and polished with soft stones and then washed with olive oil soap prior to a final waxing. The lustrous finish can range from dark brown to pinkish-red or pale tobacco.

COLOR PALETTE Most Moroccan colors derive directly from the sands and soils, which are used as a source to construct the earth bricks and which range from various shades of yellow ocher to umber and pink. The traditional fabrics utilize strong colors and stripes.

Bronze

Sunrise

Opposite The rich *tadelakt* finish is a labour-intensive process but less expensive than other opulent finishes, such as marble cladding or leather lining. The effect is completed by the textiles: the kelim, the upholstery on the chairs, and the throw on the footstool display colors and geometric patterns characteristic of North Africa.

Alluring and glamorous, bold shades create rooms with a lively and arresting atmosphere that bursts with dashing style, individuality, and spirited confidence.

saturated colors

The palette of luscious saturated colors includes strong sizzling crimsons, the scarlet of rubies and cherries, the reds of Pompeiian wall paintings, and hot Schiaparelli pinks; spicy vermilions, oranges and corals; the bright butter yellows of saffron, mangoes, and canary diamonds; the delicious verdant greens of palm trees, limes and emeralds; the savoury browns of chestnuts; ultramarine, indigo, cerulean, and sapphire blues; and the deep rich purple of violets and lavender, lilacs and amethysts. These are the exuberant and sumptuous hues whose juxtaposition can be used to add definition to architectural forms and space, including window and door frames, flights of steps and landings, terraces, shutters, fretwork screens, and bed surrounds, and to bring life to wall hangings, drapes, and bed coverings; to wooden chests, tables, and sofas; to bronze and copper lamps; to ceramic wall and floor tiles; and to the bowls and platters that are an essential of daily life in the sweltering climes of Mexico, Morocco, Turkey, Egypt, China, and India.

At the heart of the bright and vibrant palette of saturated colors lies the confident and spirited shade of red. In China, red is the color that brings forth good luck and happiness. In India the hue is associated with marriage. In most Western cultures it is the siren hue of romance, love, and valentines. Red has traditionally symbolized opulent wealth, riches, and luxury that looks back to the time when red silk damask for covering walls was the apogée of sophisticated display. Brimming with

Tangerine

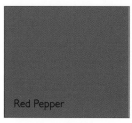

Red Pepper

COLOR PALETTE Earth colors can be subtle, like pale tobacco, or strident, like lustrous orange-red. These hot country colors look best with strong textured linens.

warmth and vitality, red gives a country-style interior a sumptuous and glowing backdrop for paintings, mirrors, furnishing textiles, and decorative artifacts such as sculptures and ceramics. The bright color brings a bold accent into a kitchen, a bedroom, or a living room in the form of a tablecloth, quilt, throw, bed hanging, or the curtains that frame a window. Touches of red can be found in a painted door, a lampshade, the upholstery of a sofa or armchair, or something as modest as a bowl of apples, a vase of red tulips, or a collection of plates.

All shades of red, from deep cranberry, burgundy, and strawberry to the robust, shocking, and dazzling shades of pink, appear luminous and radiant by soft

candlelight or firelight. Metallic accents—silver, bronze, or gold—are glittering partners with red for everything from rope tiebacks for curtains to fringes, catching the light and adding a rich glowing ambience to a country-style interior.

Festive combinations of bright, glimmering colors— vivid lime and leaf greens, fresh citrus and daffodil yellows, vivid oranges, moody blues, and violets—are natural partners with red, particularly when punctuated with sharp cool whites and soft creams. This lustrous alliance is most frequently celebrated in vivid colorwashed or painted walls; in vibrant tartans or in florid furnishing fabrics; in ceramic tiles in a host of

Above In Morocco the natural *tadelakt* walls were originally used to line the internal walls of *hammams*, or steam baths, but the technique is equally suitable for kitchens. Here the tone is a more subtle pale sandy beige, punctuated by a vibrant green tiled sink.

Above The lustrous quality of the *tadelakt* on the walls of this Moroccan bedroom varies from day into the evening, depending on the changing light.

Left In a dining room in Mexico City, a vivid palette is applied to the walls that is reminiscent of the rich color heritage of Toltec and Aztec temples and palaces. Contrasted against a white ceiling and skirting boards, the flat-plastered walls are colorwashed in an intense orange red. This is echoed in the upholstery of the robust pine dining chairs.

125

COLOR PALETTE The vibrant colors of Mexico, from a strong orange terracotta to a particularly vivid pink, are combined with fabrics in pinks, purples, oranges, reds, yellows, greens, and blues. They are inspired by the fruits, flowers, toys and clothes in a typical Mexican marketplace.

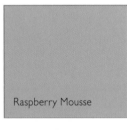

Raspberry Mousse

Electric Orange

Above and Opposite On the west coast of Mexico near Jalisco, Las Alamandas delights in the color heritage of the countryside. The colors reverberate in the strong sunlight. While subtle gradations of color, created by ragging, can be seen in the exterior paintwork, more structured pattern is introduced in the contrasting flooring, which has been laid with stone tiles and volcanic pebbles. Natural wood tones also contribute to the decorative palette. The supporting pillars, rafters, and purlins of the terrace roofs are cut from local timber and left exposed in traditional hacienda style.

Right A darker variation of *rosa Mexicana* creates a soothing backdrop to a view of the luscious vegetation—plants, bougainvillea and jasmine—an integral part of the Mexican color palette.

traditional geometric patterns that pave a kitchen floor, surround a fireplace, or embellish a tabletop; or are woven into a carpet design that features a favorite mythological or historical subject.

From polychrome striped flat-weave kelims, carpets, paisley fabrics, and madras stripes and checks to richly embroidered hangings and silken Indian saris, the scorching desert has long been a colorful accomplice for the vibrant decoration of the stucco walls and earthenware floor tiles, the soft cushions, blankets, and scatter rugs that lavishly ornament a country-style villa nestled in the suburbs of Jaipur, a tiny village in Central Africa, or in a Mexican hacienda near Puerto Vallarta. A compound of sand, quicklime, and earth-colored pigments, the lustrous *tadelakt* was traditionally used as a practical, durable, and yet sumptuous looking lining for the walls of Moroccan steam baths. Later taken up for contemporary interiors, it is a lavish example of a saturated color that has a rich heritage in a country setting.

What sets these intense, saturated colors apart is the density of the pigments that are used to achieve a deep, full-bodied richness. And the quality of light remains a key component of the captivating power of luscious and brilliant hues. In hot dry climates—from New Mexico to Tunisia and from Botswana to India—the intensity of the sunlight as it is reflected at various times of the day creates a seductive and sophisticated interplay between the luminosity of wall colors and the textures of decorative hangings and furnishing fabrics. In a modern context the distinctive palette of the desert for walls—mottled ochres, bold bright yellows, vibrant orange-reds, and mellow warm mocha browns—offset by cooling white for ceilings and the varied colors of natural building materials such as stone, marble, and wood for floors, fire surrounds, columns, and balustrades, forges a refined reinterpretation of the way that traditional rural colors were used to decorative effect, while making a bold statement when married with time-honored ornamental motifs.

Plum

Pink Haze

COLOR PALETTE Sometimes the color palette can be dominated by textiles. In both of these country homes the wall coloring is mainly off-white, but the overall impression is of rich reds, plums, and purples, and strongly graphic pattern.

Left In a modern home near Marrakesh, a traditional seating arrangement is given a completely modern twist with massive cushions in gem-like colors and blinds made from modern Moroccan textiles— the colors of the souk but with a subtle difference.

Right In Mexico designer Jenny Armit accentuated the height of the room by the use of plum below dado and off-white with a slight pink tinge above. The room is grounded by the large sofas with textured and patterned throws and cushions in tones of pink, purple, and plum.

furnishings

essential elements

IT IS THE PALETTE of colors and textures chosen to create a warm and welcoming ambience that brings the country-house interior to life. Chairs, beds, and tables; blanket chests, trunks, and closets; decorative ceramics, glass, and kitchen crockery; bedlinens, quilts and upholstery; the carpets and hooked rugs scattered across the floor, these useful necessities for day-to-day living also play a significant role in determining the colors and textures that weave a highly original and imaginative interior. Furniture and decoration that look to the pastoral ethic for inspiration best sums up the country spirit. Local materials and traditions generally determine the internal structure of a country dwelling and walls may adopt an assortment of surfaces, such as uneven limewashed stone, the soft patina of rough plasterwork, or painted brick. The appealing character of country style owes much to the simple straightforward treatment of the walls. A great wall creates a warm and inviting backdrop for the furnishings that bring individual style and a sense of history into the heart of the house.

And like the walls, floors, ceilings, and staircases, the palette of shades used for furnishings will be largely influenced by the surrounding landscape as well as by cultural traditions. Thus the glazed earthenware floor tiles and soft furnishings that enliven a hacienda in the sizzling climate of Mexico will no doubt reflect the hot, vibrant shades found in the native trees and plants of the countryside—the yellow sunflowers, bright pink bougainvillea, and green palms. In a rustic farmhouse in rural Sweden, an atmosphere of calm is created with a frosty palette of whites and creams punctuated by the pale shades of local flora—pink roses, blue harebells, yellow grasses—which is taken up for furnishing textiles, the cool timeworn patina of painted pine tables and chairs, or the tin-glazed tiles that decorate a traditional warming stove. The strong earthy colors of the fields and forests favored for an American Colonial interior crop up in the brick reds, moss greens, deep blues, and terra-cottas used for the lively patterns of brightly colored local pottery, hooked rugs, and quilted coverlets and blankets.

Treasured collections of blue-and-white ceramics, careworn copper cooking pots and pans, faded yellow woollen blankets, the warm glowing patina of elm ladderback chairs, a blanket box painted with picturesque folk patterns in shades of red and green—it is the colors of the furniture, textiles, and ceramics that bring the interior of a country-style dwelling to life .

Opposite, from top A 19th-century French white-painted *fauteuil* is given a modern twist by being upholstered in beige and strawberry velour.

An old country closet can be simply limed or painted with a rough finish to blend successfully with a country kitchen scheme.

A 19th-century ladderback chair has been given a paint finish to replicate the more fancy chairs that adorned many bedrooms of the period.

Collections of country pottery or porcelain have been regarded as the perfect accessory for country living since the beginning of the 18th century.

This charming chair, designed by Ilaria Miani, is upholstered in a hand-printed floral fabric by Rapture and Wright.

In this warm-toned Colonial room in Connecticut a 19th-century storage bin has an original craquelure finish.

Previous pages The pale gray of the walls in this Dutch sitting room, designed by Floriene Bosch, creates the soothing back-drop to the off-white painted 19th-century French sofa and the collection of textiles, from the subtle range of green and red silks to the chinoiserie inspired red embroidered off-white cotton cushions.

Right In Tuscany the table and
chairs, designed by owner Ilaria
Miani, are lacquered and painted
dark gray, mustard, and white
to mirror the tones of the
decorative wall scheme.

Below A late 19th-century
provincial open armchair in the
late-Baroque style is limed over
the natural wood.

Opposite The painted chairs in
this Tuscan farmhouse reflect the
colors of the interior, from the
pale lilac walls to the painted
cabinet to the original brick floor.

Cloudy Blue

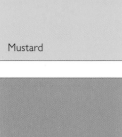

Mustard

Teal

Terra-cotta

The charm of country style living lies in its timeless appeal
and nowhere is this concept more in evidence than in the
furniture, old and new, scattered throughout the interior.

painted furniture

Although by definition country furniture is practical and
utilitarian it rarely lacks some form of ornamentation.
Many of the most ordinary and solid functional pieces
were painted in a spectrum of colors that could be found
in the vegetation of the surrounding landscape. These
pigments traditionally were applied to conceal any
deficiencies that might be present in the grain and to
camouflage timbers of inferior quality, as well as to
carry light and color into the heart of the house and often
for the sheer delight of decoration such as painting
colorful folk patterns on a blanket chest or closet.

In the spare uncluttered rooms of English and
American Colonial interiors, wall paneling and furniture
were frequently painted in deep earth tones—terra-cotta,
brick red, blue, and moss green—while the Gustavian
country style of Norway and Sweden embraced the cool,
crisp palette reflected in the surrounding terrain,
including shades of icy white, cream, celery, pale

COLOR PALETTE Country
furniture was frequently
painted as much of it was
made from inferior wood.
Traditionally this would
be done with locally
available pigments. These
natural colors are still
the most successful.

Candy Pink	Spring Green
Mist	Cloud

COLOR PALETTE Whites, off-whites, and icy grays are often accented by bright pink and a light green. Fabrics can include white cotton or linen and striped and checked cotton.

Above Gustavian-style chairs are painted in the traditional manner. The Swedish chairs were based on French salon chairs of the late 18th century, which would have been gilded. This simpler furniture, painted in tones of white, off-white, and pale gray, better suits country living.

Opposite In Sweden a common accent to the ice colors used in the interiors is pink. In this kitchen in the Stockholm house of Marianne von Kantzow of Solgården's, the pink tiles, chairs, and striped fabric are further uplifted by the use of green colorwash on the table and door architrave.

Right In a Dutch kitchen, 19th-century provincial French chairs are painted off-white.

yellow, rose pink, soft gray, and sky blue. The careworn flavor seen on many of the most engaging pieces, layers of paint that have been partly worn away, bring to light a patchwork of faded colors and raw timber. Painted furniture that has developed a scarred, worn patina over time is especially at home in a country interior, bringing a strong sense of the past while adding a cool light touch into a room. Solid, practical, and functional, country furniture has traditionally been constructed by regional craftsmen from local materials and passed down from one generation to the next.

These timeworn vernacular pieces in a host of styles from a variety of periods and a broad range of cultures happily live side by side in a country-style setting. The fine craftsmanship displayed in an American Shaker rocking chair, the rough-hewn Swedish farmhouse table enhanced by a glowing but scarred patina, or a hand-painted English comb-back Windsor chair, all bring color and life to the interior of a country-style dwelling. Yet the yearning for country simplicity might also be found in an uncluttered kitchen of minimalist design, including tables with clean lines and chairs made from natural materials such as leather and oak, or those created from man-made materials including brushed aluminum and Lucite. Whether looking back to the 18th century for

Imperial Yellow

Dragonfly

COLOR PALETTE Greens and yellows have proved perennially popular for painted country furniture. It is better to leave slightly distressed paintwork, particularly if original, rather than repaint it. Country style is forgiving of a certain amount of honest damage.

inspiration or boldly charging into the 21st century, it is the simplicity and humble character that makes up the hodgepodge of tables, chairs, and beds that lie at the heart of the country aesthetic by providing a sense of comfort and relaxation.

Almost every room in a house requires some form of seating, and it is the chair that over the centuries has answered this demand by matching the comfortable and decorative with the practical and functional. Combining straight backs with seats of leather, wicker, or rush, and the odd decorative cushion, chairs intended for the kitchen, dining room, or bedroom tend to be constructed in sturdy, durable shapes. History records that even the most plain, utilitarian country chairs and tables did not shun decoration, with flaws and imperfections inherent in the wood artfully disguised by painted patterns and designs that joyfully celebrate cultural traditions.

The chair has been a symbol of power and authority since medieval times. Tables—especially those destined for a farmhouse-inspired kitchen—tend to be the essence of simplicity, constructed of pine or oak and surrounded by homely, rush-seated chairs made in a variety of styles, from ladderback to Windsor. The tables and chairs dotted around the kitchen of a villa nestled in Tuscany or placed in an artful arrangement in the hospitable living room of a New York townhouse that has been decorated in a sleek, chic, and modern style remain both practical and decorative components to a dwelling that looks to the country for comfort, relaxation, and color.

Above Painted ladder-back chairs with rush seats have been used in country kitchens since the 18th century. They are comfortable and practical. Floral kitchen crockery on a pine farmhouse table adds to the country theme.

Right An 18th-century tripod table and ladderback chair with original paintwork are perfectly at home in an 18th-century house in Upstate New York. The 19th-century naïve artwork is another country favourite. All were sourced from antiques shops in nearby Hudson.

Opposite In the winter dining room in her Tuscan home, the designer Mimmi O'Connell has added a quaint English touch. The stacking painted garden chairs are from Winchester College and the zinc-topped table from the Conran shop.

Soft Blue

Dull Gold

COLOR PALETTE Blues were traditionally thought to encourage a restful ambience, particularly in the lighter shades, which makes them particularly suitable for bedroom furniture. They can be complemented with simple blue and white striped or check fabric or warmed by florals.

The landscape that surrounds a country dwelling plays a key role in the way chairs and tables are used to furnish and decorate an interior. As defined by the country aesthetic, they tend to be constructed in plain, clean-lined shapes and natural materials, for example, timbers such as oak, walnut, or pine that can be found in plentiful supply in the surrounding forests, or dotting the local landscape. In the roomy, commodious villas found in Palermo, Santa Fe, or Marrakesh, the demand for a cool retreat from the sizzling temperatures will inevitably create chairs and sofas painted and upholstered in light, refreshing colors—white, cream, pale yellow—or reflecting the sun-drenched colors found in the trees, plants, and flowers that make up the landscape—bright

Above Before underfloor heating, country bedrooms could be cold places, especially when the fire went out. So for practical reasons the settlers in New England copied the designs from their native Scandinavia and built enclosed beds.

Left A simple country chair is made much more attractive with a base green paint and floral embellishment. They were known in the U.S. in the 19th century as "fancy chairs."

Opposite The blue pigment in the milk-painted wooden beds brings a touch of Scandinavia to this Tuscan bedroom.

yellow, pink, and green. In the cold climates surrounding a small village in the upper reaches of Norway or Minnesota, chairs can bring additional warmth into a room when covered in rich, sumptuous shades of ruby red and persimmon, forest green and deep sapphire blue. Left natural, tables that have been constructed from timbers such as oak, pine, or elm complement the warm rich patina of wall paneling, staircases, ceiling beams, and wood plank floors. When painted in the frosty palette of the countryside, tables extend the enjoyment of daylight and add cool, crisp, color to the interior of a country dwelling.

For centuries there has been a demand for places and spaces to store, hide, and protect property. To answer this need, hutches and pantries were created for

Dewberry

Blue Gray

Chestnut

Flax

Pale Pink

COLOR PALETTE Painted closets were the essential storage unit in most country homes. Most were painted in a variety of natural pigments.

storage of food, copper pots and pans, and kitchen crockery. Racks were made to hold bottles of wine. Clothing and linens were tucked away inside cupboards. Chests and coffers furnished ample room for the brightly colored blankets and quilts designed to keep at bay the chill of a cold winter's night. Decorative caskets concealed a cache of highly prized treasures. Commodes sheltered towels, soaps and lotions. Shelves proudly housed well-read books. Glass-fronted cabinets displayed precious collections of porcelain, silver, or glass.

Throughout history country style offered a host of imaginative and resourceful solutions for storage, with forms varying by location. The architectural form of storage furniture, such as the wardrobe, was fashionable in the 17th century and continues to find favor today in refined modern interpretations or in sophisticated copies that remain true to the original. Today, the country aesthetic looks to the rural past while embracing the constant requirement for generous spaces to store belongings.

Above, left In Tuscany, a local massive late 18th– early 19th-century cupboard, with vestiges of original paint, has been adapted to become a large wardrobe.

Above, center The original two-tone paint-work on this kitchen cupboard blends well with the natural wood floor and 18th- and 19th-century furnishings and artifacts in this cottage in Upstate New York.

Above, right Many early cupboards appear to have been painted pale gray. Very often they were originally painted a much stronger color such as bright blue or green. These can be fugitive pigments which over the years fade to gray.

Opposite In this Tuscan kitchen a rather somber color scheme is brightened by the pink-painted 19th-century storage cupboard.

Warm Olive

Pale Blue

Delphinium

Deep Sea

Green-Blue

COLOR PALETTE Blues and greens were readily available pigments which were often used on painted country dressers and chests.

Wardrobes, cabinets, chests of drawers, hutches, and chests that have been constructed from local timbers in traditional vernacular shapes take center stage in country-inspired interiors. Color is achieved through decoration, the rough careworn honey-colored patina of untreated wood, or more sophisticated examples that have been used as the canvas for painted designs in soft and delicate hues such as gray, celery, cream, and blue, or lavishly embellished with brightly colored folk patterns.

Furniture made of wood is especially compatible with the rural house interior, highlighting the warmth, the comfort, and the cozy lived-in feeling that are the long-established hallmarks of the rural lifestyle. The character of a country house evolves over a period of years. It is not unusual to find sitting happily side-by-side in every room of the country interior simple homespun painted furniture that has been gathered from a variety of sources and constructed in different periods embracing a host of historic styles and decoration.

Opposite Hutches were the most useful piece of furniture in the country kitchen. Many were made from pine and were painted to correspond with the decorative scheme. Chicken wire was often applied to the cupboard doors to allow air to circulate. Here Christina Strutt of Cabbages & Roses applied a complementary red and white checked fabric backing to the doors of a sage green hutch.

Above, left Painted shelving could be used to display a family's precious objects. Even seemingly practical copper pots and pans were expensive and treasured items in the 19th century.

Above, right The original paint on the late 18th-century French closet, which is picked up in the 17th-century crewel-work hanging, inspired the decorative scheme in this country house in the Dordogne region of France.

Below, left Traditionally in Scandinavia most furniture was painted to correspond with the decor, as with this late 18th–early 19th-century longcase clock of characteristic design.

Below, right The glorious original colors of this 18th-century painted, classically inspired hutch derive from a mix of Prussian blue pigment with casein (a milk-based medium). It houses a wonderful collection of 18th- and 19th-century Scottish, English, and Irish spongeware.

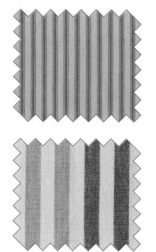

COLOR PALETTE With the main focus for color in the room coming from the textiles, linen or cotton in strong colors of sand and terra-cotta or navy and rust can be used.

The colors and textures of furnishing fabrics, from soft pale sheers to deep-toned velvets, bring warmth and comfort into the interior of a country-style dwelling. No other element is as versatile for adding depth of interest to a room.

textiles

A key source of color for a country interior lies with textiles. The soft pink and green shades of a needlework floor covering that features designs of stylized flowers; the ripe rich crimsons of Persian, Turkish, or Aubusson carpets or flat-woven kelims covering polished wooden floorboards; the cool natural tones of sisal or rush matting; or hooked or rag rugs in bright reds, yellows, and blues scattered across a stone floor will all add character and personality. There are so many ways to introduce fabrics: faded blankets, embroidered bedcovers, and handmade patchwork quilts thrown over a bed; cream-colored sheers at the windows to shelter a

Right In this essentially white environment, designer Mimmi O'Connell has introduced visual excitement by the use of fabrics. The colors were inspired by the local terrazzo floor. The fabrics are Indian cottons.

Below In Mimmi O'Connell's Tuscan home the warmth of the bedroom is due to her fabric choice. The rust and straw colors were chosen to pick up the tones in the terrazzo floor.

Right In this Tuscan guest house, designed by Piero Castellini Baldissera, the 19th-century cast iron painted daybed is covered with contrasting ticking.

Opposite The furniture and fabrics used in this Tuscan home are designed by Ilaria Miani. She was inspired by the earth tones of the local Tuscan hills.

room from the harsh rays of the sun or blue-and-white striped voile drapes hung to keep the winter chill at bay; bed coverlets and wall hangings decorated with crewelwork. Color variations are limitless, from sofa upholstery in printed calico, canvas, or woven linen boasting primary-colored checks or stripes to well-padded cushions in colorful Indian cottons, washed-out silks, or velvets. Cotton cloths and napkins can be colored in the hues of the Tuscan countryside, golden ochers and pinkish reds, or the luminous colors found in the hills of Provence, including sage greens, the sapphire blue of the sea, lemon yellows, and strong reds.

Just as colors reflect the local landscape, patterns for furnishing textiles and wallpapers look to the rural life for inspiration. Fabrics in pale soft shades of clotted creams and vanilla, leaf greens, and washed browns punctuated by occasional vibrant pea greens, bright blues, Chinese yellows, or scarlets feel at home in the rooms of a farmhouse in the cool climate of rural Upstate New York, while by contrast the interiors of sun-drenched villas located in areas that revel in warm weather all year round, such as Mexico or the deserts of Morocco, embrace cool, shimmering whites set against the rich vibrant shades found in the flowers, fruits, and palm trees of the environs. And in the Tuscan sunshine the warm-toned palette of the Italian country—yellows, ochres, pinkish reds peppered with the lavenders, blues, and greens of native flowers and herbs—is reflected in flat woven carpets, in bed covers made of cotton or linen, or in tablecloths and napkins used for a luncheon served beneath a pergola heaving with the twining tendrils of vines of climbing flowers or grapes.

COLOR PALETTE Natural earth colors in cottons and wool twills are at the heart of these country interiors. Ticking is a perennial favorite.

Indigenous flora inspire colors for textile and stencil designs, realized in bold checks and stripes, traditional florals, and provincial prints in faded cottons, linens, and ticking that lend a homespun atmosphere to sitting rooms, kitchens, and bedrooms The pioneering New Englanders and Pennsylvania Dutch settlers had a fondness for blends of deep, sumptuous colors in complementary patterns for bed coverings and quilts, window shades, and rugs. A hodgepodge of colors and textures, the bed covers, curtains, scatter rugs, and upholstery remain simple and never too self-consciously coordinated. The end result is comfort and relaxation.

At the heart of country style lays the need for a refuge, a nurturing escape from the stresses of modern life as well as from the climes of the surrounding landscape—the sizzling, sun-drenched plains of southern Spain or the cold barren hillsides of Scandinavia. The bed and the bedroom offer the perfect hideaway from everyday cares and their decorative embellishments traditionally bring rest and relaxation into this cozy sheltered space.

For centuries country-style beds have been constructed from indigenous woods, among them maple, pine, chestnut, and oak. These beds were then dressed with textiles that had been delicately embroidered with easily recognizable folk patterns, needlework motifs of flowers and foliage, or printed, painted, or woven with designs featuring colorful mythological or historical themes. Other traditional fabrics for bedspreads, bed drapes, and pelmets include quilted cottons, colorful Indian chintzes, ginghams, and toile patterns in harmonious color combinations, of blue and white, blue and red, yellow and red, or lavender and green. More modern hard-edged bed frames made from iron or brushed steel are softened by linens and cottons in shades of cream and gray.

Silk, linen, velvet, and tapestry, the rich and luxurious textiles often used for bed coverlets, bed curtains, cushion covers, and matching window curtains appear in a palette of delicious combinations of colors, crimson and hot pink, emerald and sage green, sapphire and sky blue, sunshine and daffodil yellow. The luxurious fabrics in rich

Opposite, above left In an 18th-century Dutch farmhouse in Columbia County, New York, modern seating is covered in loose covers of blue-and-white ticking to blend perfectly with the 18th- and 19th-century country furniture.

Opposite, above right Again ticking is used to great effect, in this case in a Tuscan room where all the other influences come from the Far East; the bamboo four-poster is from Bali and the horseshoe-back chairs from China.

Opposite, below left Against the background of dark-gray-and-white ticking the warm colors come from a collection of paisley pattern quilts and pillows.

Opposite, below right The striking modern cast-iron four-post bed, which was inspired by 19th-century examples, is made even more dramatic by the choice of black-and-white check bedding.

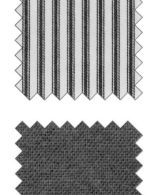

COLOR PALETTE Utility fabrics have always suited country interiors. Whether in cotton with stripes or checks of blues, pinks, black, or dark gray, or heavy linen in smokey gray or drab green, the fabrics are perfectly suited to a more relaxed interior.

Right These painted 19th-century Swedish hall chairs are covered with slate-gray linen slipcovers in this Upstate New York home.

COLOR PALETTE Pink and red cottons of all designs, whether patterned, striped, checked, or simple floral sprigs, can be combined to create a particularly feminine look.

colors elevate the bedroom to the exalted position of the most important room in a country dwelling, with the bed taking pride of place as the major piece of furniture in it.

The colors chosen for the bed coverings, quilts, pillow covers, and draperies that decorate the bedroom—in a cool and restful color palette of white, straw, celery, sky blue, and lilac to calm the senses or a warm and cozy palette made up of exotic jewel tones to excite the senses—bring the comfort of country into this intimate refuge. In a Mexican hacienda or a villa in Tuscany, the dressings of a bed—comforting quilts, clean crisp sheets, and canopy draperies—take their cue from the colors of the earth, indigenous plants, flowers, and trees. In Italy, the yellow-ocher and red-ocher, sienna, umber, and terra-cotta shades of local clays, along with the greens and browns of vines, herbs, and the cypress, oak, and chestnut trees found in woodlands combine with a palette of blues from pale sky to lavender. In Mexico the hot pinks of bougainvillea, purple of pansies, yellow of sunflowers and alamandas, and the green of cacti and palms are tempered with cool whites and creams.

Above Toiles and overall floral wallpapers and fabrics create a warm encompassing environment in a house in Provence designed by Jean-Louis Raynaud and Kenyon Kramer.

Right A late 17th-century provincial armchair is brought up to date with three slightly different red and white check gingham fabrics.

Opposite Although the toiles and simple pink and white striped fabrics hint at France, the wall color is essentially Tuscan.

The country lifestyle rarely plays host to ornament for
ornament's sake. Instead it looks to objects created with a
purpose in mind to furnish colorful and useful decoration.

ceramics

Artful displays of functional ceramics—pitchers, plates
and platters, cups and saucers, coffee pots and cream
jugs, serving bowls and soup tureens—bring pleasure and
character to an interior that has been decorated in the
rural style. In a similar vein, ceramic tableware that were
at one time useful in day-to-day life, but have long since
lost their value as functional objects, may be arranged
with an eye to celebrating not only their natural beauty
but the fine craftsmanship of years gone by as well.

Country style depends upon many things born in the
surrounding countryside to enhance the decoration of a
kitchen, a sitting room, a bedroom, or a terrace. Nowhere
is the country aesthetic more beautifully brought to life
than in the palette of colors that bring the outside in.
Folk traditions and the indigenous crafts of a culture

depend upon the hues found in the soil of the earth, in trees, and in plants and flowers to fire the imagination. Inspiration comes from the roses and harebells that grow wild in the fields of rural Scandinavia, the golden brown timbers that originate from a nearby forest and take pride of place in the ceiling beams or floor planks of a chalet nestled in the Adirondacks, or in the brick-lined kitchen floor or sun-baked roof tiles of a Mexican hacienda.

Ceramics and glass, along with furnishing textiles, demonstrate the dedicated practice of looking to these natural tones for inspiration. The soft, milky whites and off-whites known as creamware, a white ware of thin gauge with a smooth lead glaze, ousted the traditional lead-glazed earthenware as ceramic of choice for many households. Creamware was lightweight, durable, and, most importantly, inexpensive. It was created as an alternative to porcelain in the mid-18th century in Staffordshire and was then improved at the English Wedgwood factory and continues to be produced in Staffordshire today. It is ideally suited to the cool, crisp, country-inspired interiors found in northern climates, as well as in kitchens and dining rooms that have been decorated in a clean, modern Minimalist style. Although sometimes decorated with underglaze or overglaze painting or transfer printing, creamware tends to be at its most beautiful when left plain and embellished with pierced or applied decoration for added texture, for example, latticework, shell pattern-shapes, or the prunus or peony blossoms inspired by the decoration of the highly-prized *blanc de chine* porcelain vessels.

In the 18th century creamware was a key British contribution to the ceramic world and was exported and copied all over Europe. Although not rivaling the wonderful porcelains made at Meissen in Germany and Sèvres in France, creamware was the natural choice for the middle classes, particularly in the countryside. In around 1780, to compete with Chinese Export Porcelain, the basic yellowish glaze was replaced by a bluish one which became known as pearlware. Clear crystal or cut-glass ware complements the sophisticated elegance of the clean and luminous yellowish and bluish whites.

Left The soft gray tone of the painted interior of this 19th-century faux bamboo cabinet is the perfect backdrop to display a collection of 18th-century English creamware.

Left, center As cream and off-white pitchers have been produced by many factories over the years, a good collection can be easily put together. They work particularly well in the muted tones of a country kitchen.

Left, below Creamware was an overnight success for the 18th-century Staffordshire potters and they were able to produce a wide variety of shapes. Particularly desirable are tureens with covers, stands, and ladles and also the wonderful leaf dishes and sauceboats. This collection demonstrates the variation in colors that creamware covers.

Opposite Given the backdrop of a classical wallpaper, reminiscent of an 18th-century toile de Jouy, a wonderful collection of 18th-century creamware is the perfectly toned accessory.

Opposite This country kitchen in the home of Kate Dyson is a temple to blue and white. From the blue-and-white toile curtains to the floral and lace table cloth, from blue glassware to 19th- and 20th-century transferware, from blue-and-white Cornish ware to the blue detailing on the hutch, nothing is consciously matched and yet everything looks totally at home.

Pearlware continued to be made into the 19th century and was ideal for the blue transfer-printed designs produced by factories like Spode and Davenport.

The introduction of transfer-printing transformed the British porcelain industry. It meant that dinner services could be produced in large quantities as transfer-printing did away with the need for skilled hand-painting. Printed designs were usually in a single color, originally blue followed by black and then by a plethora of colors including claret brown, Gordon green, and crimson. The designs were originally inspired by the designs of the porcelains that came from China. The perennial favourite, the Willow Pattern, was developed by Josiah Spode in around 1790 from a Chinese design called Mandarin. The Willow Pattern and another chinoiserie design from this period, Asiatic Pheasants, are still in production today. In the 19th century, many of the potters took their inspiration from illustrated books and topographical engravings with views of Asia Minor, Italy, and India. As can be seen in these pages, there was tremendous interest in the African safari, including tiger hunts. In terms of collecting and displaying, the patterns produced in the 19th century offer a seemingly endless variety. Potters took advantage of the public's interests, so political satire was used on the crockery as were local British scenes with series titles such as Picturesque Scenery, British

Above The wonderful unifying theme of traditional blue-and-white ceramics means that, old or new, whatever shape or style, they always fit in perfectly with a classic country environment.

Right The English firm Spode was at the forefront of transferware. A collection works particularly well in a period oak hutch. This rather special collection is all from the highly collectable Indian Sporting Series. They were based on drawings from Captain Thomas Williamson's *Oriental Field Sports, Wild Sports of the East*, which was published in 1807.

158

Right and Below Although the Classical Antiquities series produced by Joseph Clementson, registered in 1849, was popular in blue and white, many people collect the brown-and-white alternative. There are many patterns of brown-and-white transferware available and they can prove cheaper.

Opposite The brown and white theme can be carried on into the general decor, as Stephanie Reeve has done in her Atlanta home. When pieces are used as decoration, condition does not need to be perfect. Many of these pieces, if slightly damaged, can be found in junk shops and as job lots at auction.

Views, and Antique Scenery. The Staffordshire potters were keen to open up new markets and commissioned an Irish artist, W.G.Wall, to travel to the U.S. and draw scenes that could be used on the growing export market. By the 1830s the quality of the glazes had improved substantially and it was possible to experiment with other colors, sepia and mulberry were very popular, and it was also possible to print in two or more colors. This was also the period when flow blue was introduced, a type of ceramic with a blue glaze that blurred during the firing process. It became very popular in the U.S.

Over the years the East has also inspired countless imitations of its widely admired blue-and-white

porcelain, and this also is perfectly at home in a country-style setting. As beautiful for display as for everyday use, kitchen crockery made of earthenware that has been glazed a brilliant white and painted with pastoral designs in cobalt blue looks back for inspiration to the Dutch and English delftware of the 17th century. Like creamware, it is in the cool northern climes where blue-and-white ceramics really shine. Against the chilly backdrop of a rural Scandinavian farmhouse painted in pale shades of white, cream, and gray the platters, plates, and serving dishes that reflect the blue hues of the plants and flowers growing in the surrounding countryside bring warmth into the interior. Their character is enhanced when used in concert with cozy furnishing textiles striped with blue, a fireplace surrounded with decorative blue-and white tiles, or wall paneling painted with harebells.

By contrast, country dwellings surrounded by hot, sizzling temperatures typically feature locally produced

Left and Below Collecting porcelains and pottery with a floral theme has endless possibilities. In the second half of the 19th century there was a tremendous demand for transferware and hand-painted floral wares and they were produced in many factories in Europe and the Far East. Here a small late 19th-century Bavarian porcelain vase sits next to a Chinese export vase from the same period. And in the pink painted hutch a 19th-century Staffordshire tureen and cover with aubergine transfer-printed decoration is surrounded by wares from many Staffordshire factories.

Opposite In this large Dutch white-painted closet the bright green painted interior provides the perfect background for a vast array of floral wares made in factories in Staffordshire, England, the Netherlands, and Germany.

ceramics with colorful decoration that mirrors the scorching landscape. A Mexican hacienda features the bright yellow of the alamanda flower, the hot pink of bougainvillea, and palm tree green, while a retreat in Morocco boasts earthenware vases and serving platters decorated in the rich, warm shades of burnt umber and yellow ocher found in the sands and soils of the North African desert. A farmhouse nestled in the Provençal countryside celebrates the land with faience colored in a palette of grass greens, the yellow of sunflowers, and the scarlet of poppies. In a luxurious villa in Tuscany the vibrant red, green, and yellow pigments along with dry earthy terra-cottas and ochers enliven the painted decoration of glossy tin-glazed earthenwares used every day trace their origins to the celebrated maiolica produced in Italy from the 16th century.

From Pennsylvania to Virginia, and across the Atlantic to Spain and Portugal, France and England, ceramics have played a dual role as both useful wares and everyday objects and as decorative accessories for an interior that looks to the landscape for inspiration.

Following pages: Left The pale yellow-ocher walls in the courtyard of this farmhouse, built in the 1820s near St Remy in the South of France, diffuse the bright summer sun. The verdant greens of the topiary and vines add yet more color.

Right The walls of this late 19th-century farmhouse in Tarn et Garonne, France, are built of rough local fieldstone and the door openings from local brick. Lemon trees grow in local green-glazed terra-cotta pots.

sources for paints and fabrics

NATURAL MATERIALS

Wood page 18
Adobe White
Benjamin Moore: Adobe White 2166-70
Fine Paints of Europe: SK1
Cotton
Benjamin Moore: Cottontail 2155-70
Off-white
Farrow & Ball: Pointing 2003
Drab
Fine Paints of Europe: TWI Dublin Drab

Stone page 27
Cannon
Farrow & Ball: Downpipe 26
Fine Paints of Europe: SK36
Tin
Farrow & Ball: Hardwick White 5
Benjamin Moore: Shale 861
Smokey
Fine Paints of Europe: CG61
Farrow & Ball: Pigeon 25
Mortar
Fine Paints of Europe: SK10

Earth page 30
Pink Rose
Benjamin Moore: Rose Bisque 2102-05
Faded Pink
Farrow & Ball: Red Earth 64
Fine Paints of Europe: CG-21
Sand
Farrow & Ball: Print Room Yellow 69
Benjamin Moore: Beverley Hills 180
Desert Dust
Farrow & Ball: Archive 227
Benjamin Moore: King Arthur's Court
    1081

PAINTS AND PIGMENTS

Page 34
Lemon
Benjamin Moore: Lemon Drops 2019-50
Corn
Farrow & Ball: Babouche 223
Benjamin Moore: Broadway Lights 298
Sienna
Benjamin Moore: Bryce Canyon 098

Page 37
Mud
Benjamin Moore: Spanish Red 1301
Tobacco
Benjamin Moore: Beaver Brown 2104-20

Page 39
Calico
Farrow & Ball: Cream 44
Benjamin Moore: Blond Wood 1067
Fine Paints of Europe: LP-22
Peanut
Benjamin Moore: Peanut Shell 2162-40

Egg Yolk
Benjamin Moore: Marblehead Gold
    HC-11
Fine Paints of Europe: CG-1

Page 40
Linen
Benjamin Moore: Frappe AF-85
Farrow & Ball: Clunch 2009
Sunbeam
Benjamin Moore: Sun Porch 2023-30

Page 43
Honey
Benjamin Moore: Sweet Orange
    2017-40
Nectar
Benjamin Moore: Sweet Nectar 156

Page 44
Frost Blue
Benjamin Moore: Oystershell 864
Sea
Benjamin Moore: Silent Night 1613
Lichen
Benjamin Moore: Scenic Drive 697

Page 47
Crocus
Benjamin Moore: Crocus 1404
Coral
Benjamin Moore: Antique Coral 1198

COOL COLORS

Whites and Off-Whites
Page 53
Paint
Pure White
Farrow & Ball: All White 2005
Benjamin Moore: Pure White
Owl
Benjamin Moore: Owl Gray 06-52
Farrow & Ball: Pavilion Gray 242
Stone
Farrow & Ball: Stoney Ground 211
Benjamin Moore: Stone Hearth 984
Fine Paints of Europe: AR-1
Fabric
GP&J Baker, Threads, Cumulus, Dove
    ED85071 910
Roger Oates, Riva, 2033 Natural

Page 55
Paint
Pigeon
Farrow & Ball: Pigeon 25
Benjamin Moore: Sage Mountain 1488
Atlantic
Benjamin Moore: Pebble Beach 1597
Fabric
De la Cuona, Mistral Stone, MIS2
De la Cuona, Jackdaw Steel, JAC2

Page 56
Paint
Peace
Benjamin Moore: Dove Wing OC-18
Buttermilk
Benjamin Moore: Devon Cream
    OC-102
Lotus
Benjamin Moore: Pink Damask OC-72
Fabric
Linum, Ios C19
Calico Corners, Ticking, Linen/Black

Page 59
Paint
Dillweed
Benjamin Moore: Crownsville Gray
    HC-106
Mink
Farrow & Ball: Old White 4
Benjamin Moore: Sag Harbour Gray
    HC-95
Fine Paints of Europe: AR-3
Dusty Pink
Farrow & Ball: Calamine 230
Benjamin Moore: Touch of Pink
    2008-70
Fabric
Linum, Desiree D90

Creams and Pale Yellows
Page 60
Paint
Oatmeal
Farrow & Ball: Off White 3
Benjamin Moore: Indian White OC-88
Sherbet
Farrow & Ball: Lancaster Yellow 249
Benjamin Moore: San Pedro
    Morning 366
Fine Paints of Europe: SK-25
Fabric
Ian Mankin, Suffolk Check S, Bluebell

Page 63
Paint
Tallow
Farrow & Ball: Tallow 203
Benjamin Moore: Canvas 267
Fine Paints of Europe: AR-19
Vanilla
Farrow & Ball: Matchstick
Fine Paints of Europe: LP-24
Red Earth
Farrow & Ball: Terre D'Egypt 247
Benjamin Moore: Segovia Red 1288
Fabric
Dominique Kieffer, Sauvage,
    Lin 17117-004

Page 64
Paint
Cream
Benjamin Moore: Light Yellow 2022-60
Farrow & Ball: Lancaster Yellow 249
Duck Egg
Benjamin Moore: Brittany Blue 1633
Fabric
Jane Churchill, Allen Check, Blue J567F/01
Ralph Lauren, Dishtowel Stripe Blue
    (available at Calico Corners)

Page 67
Paint
Lemon Ice
Benjamin Moore: Lemon Meringue 2023-50
Off-Black
Farrow & Ball: Off-Black 57
Fine Paints of Europe: SK-36
Fabric
Dominique Kieffer, Sauvage,
    Fer 17117-006
Dominique Kieffer, Oseille Sauvage,
    Souris 17075-011

Greens
Page 68
Paint
Willow
Farrow & Ball: Vert de Terre 234
Benjamin Moore: Aganthus Green 470
Gray-Green
Farrow & Ball: Castle Gray 92
Fine Paints of Europe: CG-59
Lavender
Benjamin Moore: Lavender 2070-60
Fabric
Osborne & Little, Skye Linen F5680/09

Page 71
Paint
Leaf
Benjamin Moore: Leisure Green 2035-60
Fine Paints of Europe: AR-7
Forest
Benjamin Moore: Stokes Forest Green
    2035-40
Vermillion
Farrow & Ball: Blazer 212
Benjamin Moore: Moroccan Red 1309
Fabric
Calico Corners, Granny, Black

Page 72
Paint
Arsenic
Farrow & Ball: Arsenic 214
Benjamin Moore: Southfield Green HC-129
Mint
Benjamin Moore: Soft Mint 2041-60
Fine Paints of Europe: AR-4

Storm
Farrow & Ball: Hague Blue 30
Benjamin Moore: New York State of
Mind 805
Fabric
Lena Proudlock, Denim, Pale Green

Page 75
Paint
Rich Jade
Benjamin Moore: Weeping Willow 629
Farrow & Ball: Calke Green 34
Folly
Farrow & Ball: Olive 13
Benjamin Moore: Rolling Hills 1497
Olive
Benjamin Moore: Grassy Fields 2034-30
Grass
Farrow & Ball: Folly Green 76
Benjamin Moore: Harrisburg Green
HC-132
Fabric
Calico Corners, Fairbanks, Floral
Nobilis, Rayure Gatsby, 8910.94

Cool Blues
Page 77
Paint
Winter Blue
Benjamin Moore: Sea View 836
Fog
Benjamin Moore: Jet Stream 814
Fine Paints of Europe: SK-28
Ice
Benjamin Moore: Sapphire Ice 808

Page 79
Paint
Forget-Me-Not
Benjamin Moore: Windmill Wings
2067-60
Fine Paints of Europe: SK-28
Hyacinth
Benjamin Moore: Freesia 1432
Fired Earth: Sea Lavender 86
Dark Blue
Benjamin Moore: Blueberry Hill 812
Farrow & Ball: Drawing Room Blue 253
Fabric
Vintage Denim

Page 80
Paint
Nordic Blue
Benjamin Moore: Blue Dragon 810
Sky
Benjamin Moore: Soft Sky 807
Ivory White
Benjamin Moore: Ivory White 925
Fine Paints of Europe: SK-6
Blush
Benjamin Moore: Gentle Blush
2084-70
Fine Paints of Europe: CG-36

Fabric
Calico Corners, Toile, Central Park,
Red
Elanbach, Hay Buff, 04 Stone

Grays
Page 82
Paint
Light Gray
Farrow & Ball: Pavilion Gray 242
Fine Paints of Europe: AR-3
Gustavian Gray
Benjamin Moore: Blue Heather 1620
Thundercloud
Benjamin Moore: Thundercloud Gray
2124-40
Fabric
Linum, Stone 10H, Design:
Synnöve Mork

Page 84
Paint
Silver Streak
Benjamin Moore: Silver Streak
2119-400
Steel
Benjamin Moore: Sweatshirt Gray
2126-40
Cashmere
Benjamin Moore: Gray Cashmere
2138-60
Fine Paints of Europe: AR-9
Heath
Benjamin Moore: Heather Gray
2139-40
Fabric
GP&J Baker, Threads, Cumulus,
Polar ED85071 100

Page 86
Paint
Lead
Benjamin Moore: Lead Gray 2131-30
Farrow & Ball: Railings 31
Crimson
Farrow & Ball: Incarnadine 248
Benjamin Moore: My Valentine 1330
Fabric
Dominique Kieffer, Tissage de Coton,
Petrole 17106-010
De La Cuona, Desert Cloth White, BD4

WARM COLORS
Yellow Earth Tones
Page 91
Paint
Toffee Cream
Farrow & Ball: Farrow's Cream 67
Benjamin Moore: Porter Ranch
Cream 148
Cord
Farrow & Ball: Cat's Paw 240
Benjamin Moore: Spice Gold 1040

Fabric
Chelsea Textiles Ltd, FC401
Small Tea Check

Page 92
Paint
Straw
Farrow & Ball: Straw 52
Benjamin Moore: Tucson Tan 1144
Fine Paints of Europe: AR-11
Wheat
Benjamin Moore: Wheatfield 2159-50
Fabric
Donghia, Maestro Windows, Oatmeal
10097-98
Donghia, Garrett Leather, Avion 280
Canyon '01

Page 94
Paint
Sunbeam
Benjamin Moore: Sun Porch 2023-30
Burgundy
Benjamin Moore: Dark Burgundy
2075-10
Farrow & Ball: Brinjal 222
Fabric
Malabar, Kelso 07
Calico Corners, McGee Guncheck,
Moss

Page 97
Paint
Sunshine
Benjamin Moore: Sunshine 2021-30
Sunflower
Flamant: CC404 Judorange
Benjamin Moore: Semolina 2155-40
French Gray
Farrow & Ball: French Gray 18
Fine Paints of Europe: LP-19
Fabric
Lee Jofa, Kirtan Stripe, Petal 2006137

Page 98
Paint
Candlelight
Benjamin Moore: Candlelit Dinner 295
Farrow & Ball: Dayroom Yellow 233
Nacho
Benjamin Moore: Nacho Cheese
2018-40
Citrus Burst
Benjamin Moore: Citrus Blast 2018-30
Fabric
Calico Corners, Stripe/Azalea

Red Earth Tones
Page 100
Paint
Warm White
Farrow & Ball: Wimborne White 239
Benjamin Moore: Maritime White
OC-5

Colonial Red
Farrow & Ball: Eating Room Red 43
Fabric
Donghia, Mummy's Cloth 7950,
01 Currant
Mulberry Home, Floral Roccoco,
Taupe FD101/523N101

Page 103
Paint
Rich Red
Farrow & Ball: Incarnadine 248
Benjamin Moore: Moroccan Red 1309
Benjamin Moore: My Valentine 1330
Rouge
Benjamin Moore: Rouge 2084-30
Farrow & Ball: Rectory Red 217
Rose
Benjamin Moore: Rosy Glow 2084-50
Fine Paints of Europe: CG-31
Battleship
Farrow & Ball: Downpipe 26
Benjamin Moore: Dark Pewter 2122-10

Page 104
Paint
Tomato
Benjamin Moore: Rosy Apple 2006-30
Pepper
Benjamin Moore: Ansonia Peach
HC-52
Tuscan Olive
Fine Paints of Europe: SK-20
Marlin
Benjamin Moore: Silver Marlin
2139-50
Fine Paints of Europe: SK-32
Fabric
Malabar, Carom 37

Warm Blues
Page 106
Paint
Summer Sky
Benjamin Moore: Summer Blue
2067-50
Lapis
Benjamin Moore: Blue Lapis 2067-40
Soft Violet
Benjamin Moore: Softened Violet 1420
Fabric
Malabar, Ipanema 03, IPAN03

Page 109
Paint
Blue Lagoon
Benjamin Moore: True Blue 2066-50
Violet
Benjamin Moore: Persian Violet 1419
Brazilian
Benjamin Moore: Brazilian Blue 817
Farrow & Ball: Cook's Blue 237
Island Green
Benjamin Moore: Neptune Green 658

Fabric
Cabbages & Roses, Mama Red

Page 111
Paint
Island Blue
Benjamin Moore: Honolulu Blue
  2066-60
Farrow & Ball: Blue Ground 210
Lake Blue
Benjamin Moore: Blue Lapis 2067-40
Fabric
Linum, Nisha C07

HOT COLORS
Flower Power
Page 114
Paint
Rose Pink
Benjamin Moore: Bayberry 2080-50
Sunset
Benjamin Moore: Island Sunset 1346
Fabric
GP&J Baker, Seasons Silk, Fuchsia,
  BP10149
Jane Churchill, Fontwell Check,
  J418F-04 Pink

Page 117
Paint
Desert Sky
Benjamin Moore: Rocky Mountain Sky
  2066-40
Blue Sea
Benjamin Moore: Sea to Shining Sea
  789789
Fabric
Jane Churchill, Alston Weave,
  J172F-04 Blue
GP&J Baker, Provence Toile,
  Green/Blue 121403

Page 118
Paint
Lime Green
Benjamin Moore: Lime Green
  2026-1000
Evergreen
Benjamin Moore: Sullivan Green 560
Fabric
Calico Corners, Charleston/Spring
Cabbage & Roses, French Toile,
  Raspberry 0602 R045 048 69
Jane Churchill, Arcadia, Pink/Lime
  J514F/01

Page 121
Paint
Viper Green
Benjamin Moore: Paradise Valley 559
Indian Rose
Benjamin Moore: Razzle Dazzle 1348

Bold Orange
Benjamin Moore: Racing Orange
  2169-10
Fabric
Parkertex, Sanibel, Magenta/Gold,
  PF50025
Malabar, Yasmin 01, YASM01

Saturated Colors
Page 122
Paint
Bronze
Benjamin Moore: Bronze Tone 2166
Sunrise
Benjamin Moore: Fiesta Orange 084
Fabric
Mulberry Home, Halcyon Stripe,
  Red/Brick FD635 V127
Donghia, Righe 9305-01 Vino

Page 124
Paint
Tangerine
Benjamin Moore: Tangerine Melt 091
Red Pepper
Benjamin Moore: Pinata 007
Fabric
Lee Jofa, Groundworks, David Hicks
  by Ashley Hicks, Coggeshall Solid,
  Claret 2443-GWF 9

Page 126
Paint
Raspberry Mousse
Benjamin Moore: Raspberry Mousse
  2076-40
Electric Orange
Benjamin Moore: Electric Orange
  2015-10
Fabric
Mulberry Home, Trio Velvet Stripe,
  Pink FD617 W28
Malabar, Bamboo Sorrel, BAM274
Donghia, Tamal 10053, Pastilla

Page 128
Paint
Plum
Benjamin Moore: Chinaberry 1351
Farrow & Ball: Rectory Red No.217
Pink Haze
Benjamin Moore: Purple Cream
  2073-70
Farrow & Ball: Middleton Pink 245
Fabric
Malabar, Siam 34, SIAM34
GP&J Baker, Threads, Infinity, Brown
  ED85002

FURNISHINGS
Painted Furniture
Page 134
Paint
Cloudy Blue
Benjamin Moore: Instinct AF-575
Farrow & Ball: Parma Gray 27
Mustard
Benjamin Moore: American Cheese
  2019-40
Teal
Benjamin Moore: Jamestown Blue
  HC-148
Farrow & Ball: Chappell Green No.83
Terra-cotta
Benjamin Moore: Golden Gate 033

Page 137
Paint
Candy Pink
Benjamin Moore: Full Bloom 2001-50
Spring Green
Benjamin Moore: Killala Green 558
Mist
Benjamin Moore: Seattle Gray 2130-70
Farrow & Ball: Blackened 2001
Cloud
Benjamin Moore: Mt. Rainier Gray
  2129-60

Page 138
Paint
Imperial Yellow
Benjamin Moore: Imperial Yellow 314
Dragonfly
Benjamin Moore: Dragonfly AF-510
Farrow & Ball: Minster Green 224

Page 141
Paint
Soft Blue
Benjamin Moore: Soft Jazz 809
Dull Gold
Benjamin Moore: Bright Gold 371

Page 142
Paint
Dewberry
Benjamin Moore: Old Blue Jeans 839
Blue Gray
Benjamin Moore: Airway 828
Chestnut
Benjamin Moore: New Chestnut AC-6
Flax
Benjamin Moore: Weston Flax HC-5
Farrow & Ball: Hound Lemon No.2
Fine Paints of Europe: TW2-Savannah
Pale Pink
Benjamin Moore: Romantic Pink
  2004-70
Fine Paints of Europe: CG-36

Page 144
Paint
Warm Olive
Benjamin Moore: Hiking Path 524
Pale Blue
Benjamin Moore: Serenata AF-535
Delphinium
Benjamin Moore: French Violet 1427
Deep Sea
Benjamin Moore: Sailor's Sea Blue
  2063-40
Green-Blue
Benjamin Moore: Varsity Blues 7565

Textiles
Page 146
Fabric
Calico Corners, Ticking, Walnut
Calico Corners, Williamsburg,
  Spotswood Stripe/Jewel
Malabar, Mahe 02, MAHE02

Page 149
Fabric
Folia, Philippe Stripe, Camel/Rouge
  (available at Calico Corners)
Lee Jofa, Groundworks, David Hicks
  by Ashley Hicks, Axum Stripe,
  Natural 2431-GWF 16
Jane Churchill, Allen Check,
  Beige J567F/02
Mulberry Home, London Check,
  Pink/Green FD542

Page 151
Fabric
Top left:
GP&J Baker, Provence Stripe,
  Delft J0613
Top right:
Calico Corners, Classic Ticking, Black
Bottom left:
Ian Mankin, Suffolk Checks Black
Bottom right:
Mulberry Home,
  Heavy Linen, Smokey Grey

Page 152
Fabric
Top left:
GP&J Baker, Provence Toile,
  Pink R1403
Top right:
Cabbages & Roses, Bees
Bottom left:
Romo, New Haversham, Wickham
  Pomegranate 7223/33
Bottom right:
Ian Mankin, Candy Stripe Peony

directory

Architects and Designers

Abraham & Thakore Ltd.
C 21, Sector 4
NOIDA 201301
India
+91 120 2519583
+91 120 2519584
+91 120 2519585
www.abrahamandthakore.com

Las Alamandas
Km. 83 Carretera Federal, #200
Quemaro, Costalegre
Jalisco 48980
Mexico
www.alamandas.com

Alexandra Champalimaud & Associates
One Union Square West, #705
New York, NY 10003
212 807 8869
www.alexchamp.com

Angie Hranowsky Design Studio
2037 Lakeshore Drive
Charleston, SC 29412
843 810 3286
www.angiehranowsky.com

Annsley Interiors
617 413 3173
annsley@annsleyinteriors.com
www.annsleyinteriors.com

Archaeo Architects
1519 Upper Canyon Road, Studio A
Santa Fe, NM 87501
505 820 7200
www.archaeoarchitects.com

Jenny Armit
The Hotelito
Rancho de la Cachora
Todos Santos BCS 23305
Mexico
+52 612 145 0099
www.thehotelito.com

Axel Vervoordt
Castle Gravenwezel
St. Jobsteenweg 64
B-2970s-Gravenwezel
Belgium
+32 03 658 1470
www.axel-vervoordt.com

Paula Baker-Laporte
PO Box 864
Tesuque, NM 87574
505 989 1813
www.bakerlaporte.com

Piero Castellini Baldissera
Via Morozzo della Rocca 5
20123 Milano
Italy
+39 02 469 2068

Barbara Davis
607 264 3673
www.bdavisdesigner.com

Beckwith Interiors
6025 Highway 100
Nashville, TN 37205
615 356 0808
www.beckwithinteriors.com

Bed of Flowers
Floriene Bosch
Dijk 45
6651 LA Beuningen
Belgium
+31 024 675 0849
www.bedofflowers.nl

Betty Burgess Design
3209 Paces Ferry Place NW
Atlanta, GA 30305
404 841 7707

Bilhuber & Associates
330 East 59th Street, 6th Floor
New York, NY 10022
212 308 4888
www.bilhuber.com

Patrick Clifford
Architectus
PO Box 1401, Shortland Street
Auckland 1140
New Zealand
+64 9 307 5970
www.architectus.com.au

Anthony Collett
Collett-Zarzycki
Fernhead Studios
2B Fernhead Road
London W9 3ET
United Kingdom
+44 020 8969 6967
www.collett-zarzycki.com

Dominique Kieffer
Les Editions Dominique Kieffer
6bis, rue de L'Abbaye
75006 Paris
France
+33 15 681 2020
www.dkieffer.com

Agnes Emery
27, rue de L'Hopital
1000 Brussels
Belgium
+32 2 513 5892
www.emeryetcie.com

Emma Jane Pilkington Fine Interiors
212 644 0248
emma@emmajanepilkington.com
www.emmajanepilkington.com

Frank Faulkner
10 S. 4th St.
Hudson, NY 12534
518 828 2295
www.frankfaulkner.com

Heiberg Cummings Design
420 W. 25th Street, #1C
New York, NY 10001
212 337 2030
www.hcd3.com

Helene Forbes-Hennie
Hennie Interiors
Thomles Gate 4
0270 Oslo
Norway
+47 22 06 8586

The Homestead LC
US Route 220 Main Street
PO Box 2000
Hot Springs, VA 24445
540 839 1766
www.thehomestead.com

Ilaria Miani
Via Monserrato 35
00186 Rome
Italy
+39 06 683 3160
www.ilariamiani.tin.it

Isabelle de Borchgrave
24, rue Lens
B-1050 Brussels
Belgium
+32 2 648 5350
www.isabelledeborchgrave.com

Jacquelynne P. Lanham Designs
472 E. Paces Ferry Road NE
Atlanta, GA 30305
404 364 0472

Javier Sordo Madaleno
Paeso de la Reforma, #2076A
Lomas de Chapueltepec
Mexico City 11000
Mexico

Jennifer Flanders, Inc.
177 E. 70th Street
New York, NY 10021
646 368 1404
www.jenniferflanders.com

Johnny Grey Studios
154 South Rose Street
Mount Clemens, MI 48043
888 902 8860
www.johnnygray.com

Julie Prisca
46, rue du Bac
75007 Paris
France
+33 01 4548 1329
www.julieprisca.com

Karim El Achak
7, rue de la Liberté
Marrakesh 40000
Morroco
+212 2444 7313

Kathryn M. Ireland
1714 18th Street
Santa Monica, CA 90404
310 399 0300
www.kathrynireland.com

Kenyon Kramer
Décoration Jardin
Place des 3 Ormeaux
13100 Aix-en-Provence
France
+33 44 223 5232

Ebba Lopez
Linum France
Zone d'aménagement concerté Le
Tourail
84660 Coustellet
France
+33 49 076 3400
www.linum-france.com

Lucas Studio, Inc.
636-A North Almont Drive
West Hollywood, CA 90069
310 858 6884
www.lucasstudioinc.com

Debra Martinson
DM Interiors
3020 St. Albans Mill Rd.
Minnetonka, MN 55305
952 545 5351

Michael S. Smith
1646 19th Street
Santa Monica, CA 90404
310 315 3018
www.michaelsmithinc.com

Mimmi O'Connell
8 Eaton Square
London SW1W 9DB
United Kingdom
+44 020 7752 0474
www.mimmioconnell.com

Naomi Leff & Associates
12 W. 27th Street, #18
New York, NY 10001
212 686 6300

Paolo Badesco
Viale di porta vercellina 5
20133 Milano
Italy
+39 02 48 10 0737
www.paolobadesco.it

Paysage
3451 Fairmont Blvd.
Cleveland Heights, OH
216 397 8700
www.paysage.com

Gilles Pellerin & Nicolette Schouten
Collection Privée
9, rue des Etat-Unis
06400 Cannes
France
+33 49 706 9494
www.collection-privee.com

Silvio Rech & Lesley Carstens
+27 0 11 486 1525

Reynal Interiors
515 418 8715
reynalinteriors@att.net

John Saladino
200 Lexington Avenue, #1600
New York, NY 10016
212 684 6805
www.saladinostyle.com

Stephen Skinner
Riyad Edward
Derb Marestane 10
Zaouia Abbassia
Marrakesh 40000
Morocco
+212 524 389 797
http://www.riyadedward.com

Solis Betancourt
1739 Connecticut Avenue, NW
Washington, DC 20009
202 659 8734
www.solisbetancourt.com

Stephanie Stokes, Inc.
420 Park Avenue
New York, NY 10022
212 879 1624
www.stephaniestokesinc.com

Studio KO
7, rue Geoffroy L'Angevin
75004 Paris
France
+33 01 4271 1392
www.studioko.fr

Susan Dowhower Interiors
404 355 8506
sdowhower@bellsouth.net

Dar Tamsna Villa Marrakesh
Route de Fes Douar Tamsna
Tamsna Rue
Marrakesh 40000
Morocco
www.tamsna.com

Todhunter Earle
Chelsea Reach
79-89 Lots Road, 1st Floor
London SW10 0RN
United Kingdom
+44 020 7349 9999
www.todhunterearle.com

Tricia Foley
212 348 0074
tricia@triciafoley.com
www.triciafoley.com

Vallone Design
7707 East Third Avenue
Scottsdale, AZ 85251
480 421 2799
www.vallonedesign.com

Woodson & Rummerfield's House of
Design
8285 W Sunset Blvd., #9
West Hollywood, CA 90046
310 659 0850
www.wandrdesign.com

Paint

Auro Organic Paints
+44 014 5277 2020
www.auro.co.uk

Benjamin Moore
info@benjaminmoore.com
www.benjaminmoore.com

Bleu de Pastel de Lectoure
+33 05 6268 7830
www.bleu-de-lectoure.com

Cath Kidston
+44 014 8043 1415
www.cathkidston.co.uk

Cole & Son
+44 020 7376 4628
www.cole-and-son.com

Color Wheel Paint
407 293 6810
800 749 6810
www.colorwheelpaint.com

Craig & Rose
+44 087 0600 1829
www.craigandrose.com

Crown Paint
+44 087 0240 1127
www.crownpaint.co.uk

Dulux
www.duluxpaints.com

Earth Born
+44 019 2873 4171
www.earthbornpaints.co.uk

Emery & Cie
+32 2 513 5892
www.emeryetcie.com

Farrow & Ball
888 511 1121
www.farrow-ball.com

Fine Paints of Europe
800 332 1556
www.finepaintsofeurope.com

Fired Earth
+44 012 9581 2088
www.firedearth.com

Flamant
+32 5376 8021
www.flamantpaint.com

Francesca's Paint Ltd.
+44 020 7228 7694
www.francescaspaint.com

Hammerite
+44 087 0444 1111
www.hammerite.com

Harris
+0094 11 2859132
+0094 11 2830020
+0094 11 5671055 8
www.harrisbrushes.lk

Heritage Paints
www.heritagepaints.co.uk

Kelly Hoppen Paints
+44 020 7471 3350
www.kellyhoppenretail.com

Leyland Trade
+44 019 2435 4000
www.leyland-paints.co.uk

Marston & Langinger
212 710 5615
www.marston-and-langinger.com

Martha Stewart
888 4 MARTHA (627842)
www.marthastewart.com

The Old Fashioned Milk Paint
Company
978 448 6336
www.milkpaint.com

Old Village Paints
800 498 7687
www.old-village.com

Paint & Paper Library
+44 020 7823 7755
www.paintlibrary.co.uk

Paper & Paints
+44 020 7352 8626
www.papers-paints.co.uk

Plascon
+44 086 0204 060
www.plascon.co.za

Ralph Lauren Paint
888 475 7674
www.rlhome.polo.com

Rose of Jericho
+44 019 3583 676
www.rose-of-jericho.demon.co.uk

Sherwin-Williams
800 4 SHERWIN (7437946)
www.sherwin-williams.com

Sun Wallpaper & Paint
845 471 2880
www.sunwallpaperandpaint.com

Sydney Harbour Paint Company
213 291 1586
www.sydneyharbourpaints.com

Fabric

Abbott & Boyd Ltd.
+44 020 7351 9985
www.abbottandboyd.co.uk

Ainsworth-Noah
800 669 3512
www.ainsworth-noah.com

Alexander Beauchamp
+01254 668185
www.alexanderbeauchamp.com

Andrew Martin
212 688 4498
www.andrewmartin.co.uk

Beacon Hill
800 333 3777
www.beaconhilldesign.com

Beaumont & Fletcher
+44 020 7352 5594
www.beaumontandfletcher.com

Bergamo Fabrics
914 665 0800
www.bergamofabrics.com

Boussac
212 421 0534
www.boussacfadini.com

Brentano, Inc.
847 657 8481
www.brentanofabrics.com

Brimar
800 274 1205
www.brimarinc.com

Brunschwig & Fils, Inc.
914 684 5800
www.brunschwig.com

Cabbages and Roses
+44 020 7352 7333
www.cabbagesandroses.com

Calico Corners
800 213 6366
www.calicocorners.com

Celia Birtwell
+44 020 7221 0877
www.celiabirtwell.com

Chase Erwin Silks
+44 020 8875 1222
www.chase-erwin.com

Chelsea Textiles
212 319 5804
www.chelseatextiles.com

Claremont Furnishing Fabrics Co. Ltd.
212 486 1252
www.claremontfurnishing.com

Clarence House
800 221 4704
www.clarencehouse.com

Colefax and Fowler
+44 020 7244 7427
www.colefax.com

Cowtan & Tout
212 647 6900
www.cowtan.com

Création Baumann
+41 062 919 6262
www.creationbaumann.com

Crowson
516 293 2000
www.crowsonfabrics.com

Crucial Trading
+01562 743 747
www.crucial-trading.com

De Le Cuona
+44 020 7584 7677
www.delecuona.co.uk

Dedar
+39 031 228 7511
www.dedar.com

Dominique Kieffer
+33 1 56 81 20 20
www.dkieffer.com

Donghia, Inc.
914 662 2377
www.donghia.com

Eastern Accents
800 397 4556
www.easternaccents.com

G P & J Baker
+44 012 0226 6700
www.gpjbaker.com

Harlequin
+44 084 4543 0200
www.harlequin.uk.com

Ian Mankin
+44 020 7722 0997
www.ianmankin.com

Jane Piper Reid & Company
206 621 9290
www.jprco.com

Kravet, Inc.
516 293 2000
www.kravet.com

Lee Jofa
800 453 3563
www.leejofa.com

Lena Proudlock
+44 016 6650 0051
www.lenaproudlock.co.uk

Madura
617 267 0222
www.madura.co.uk

Malabar
+44 020 7501 4200
www.malabar.co.uk

Manuel Canovas
+44 020 7318 6000
www.manuelcanovas.com

Mulberry
+44 020 7352 3173
www.mulberryhome.com

Nina Campbell
+44 020 7225 1011
www.ninacampbell.com

Nobilis
+44 020 8767 0774
www.nobilis.fr

Olivier Desforges
800 322 3911 ext. 360
www.olivierdesforges.com

Osborne & Little
212 751 3333
www.osborneandlittle.com

Pindler & Pindler, Inc.
805 531 9090
www.pindler.com

Pollack
212 627 7766
www.pollackassociates.com

Rapture & Wright
+44 016 0865 2442
www.raptureandwright.co.uk

Rogers & Goffigon Ltd.
212 888 3242

Romo
+44 016 2375 6699
www.romofabrics.com

Rubelli
+44 020 7349 1590
www.rubelli.com

Sahco Hesslein
+49 0911 99870
www.sahcohesslein.com

Sanderson
800 894 6185
www.sanderson-uk.com

Scalamandré
631 467 8800
www.scalamandre.com

Schumacher
800 523 1200
www.fschumacher.com

Stark & Texture/Stark Carpet
212 752 9000
www.starkcarpet.com

Storehouse
888 786 7346
www.storehouse.com

Tobias and the Angel
+44 020 8878 8902
www.tobiasandtheangel.com

Travis & Company
404 237 5079
www.travisandcompany.com

Turnell & Gigon
+44 020 7259 7280
www.tandggroup.com

Warner Fabrics
+49 0617 163 202
www.warnerfabrics.com

Zimmer + Rohde
+49 0617 163 202
www.zimmer-rohde.com

Zoffany
201 399 0500
www.zoffany.com

Zuber
+33 3 8944 1388
www.zuber.fr

Furniture & Accessories

Alfies Antiques Market
+44 020 7723 6066
www.alfiesantiques.com

Andrew Dando
+44 012 2586 5444
www.andrewdando.co.uk

Anthropologie
800 309 2500
www.anthropologie.com

Artefacto
404 926 0004
www.artefacto.com

Baker
800 592 2537
www.kohlerinteriors.com

Beaumont & Fletcher
+44 020 7352 5594
www.beaumontandfletcher.com

Blanc d'Ivoire
+33 0153 38 97 00
www.blancdivoire.com

Bretz
+49 06727 89 50
www.mycultsofa.com

Bungalow Furniture & Accessories
480 948 5409
www.bungalowaz.com

The Country Seat
+44 014 9164 1349
www.thecountryseat.com

Decorative Crafts
800 431 4455
www.decorativecrafts.com

Dedon
+49 041 31 22 44 7 0
www.dedon.de

Designers Guild
203 359 1500
www.designersguild.com

Devonia Antiques for Dining
561 429 8566
www.devonia-antiques.com

Donghia, Inc.
914 662 2377
www.donghia.com

Europa Antiques
805 969 4989
www.antiqueseuropa.com

Fay Gold Gallery
404 233 3843
www.faygoldgallery.com

Galerie Frédéric Méchiche
+33 14 278 7828

Gillian Neale Antiques
+44 012 9642 3754
www.gilliannealeantiques.co.uk

Guinevere
+44 020 7736 2917
www.guinevere.co.uk

Harbinger
310 858 6884
www. harbingerla.lucasstudioinc.com

John Howard at Heritage
+44 019 9381 2580
www.antiquepottery.co.uk

Huntington Antiques
+44 014 5183 0842
www.huntington-antiques.com

Ilaria Miani
+39 06 683 3160
www.ilariamiani.it

Ixcasala
+33 06 19 33 83 93
www.ixcasala.com

JAB International Furnishing Ltd.
+44 020 7349 9323
www.jab.de

Janus et Cie
212 752 1117
www.janusetcie.com

John Bly
+44 014 4282 3030
www.johnbly.com

Josephine Ryan Antiques & Interiors
+44 020 8675 3900
www.josephineryanantiques.co.uk

Marianne von Kantzow
Solgården
+46 08 663 9360

The Kellogg Collection
202 363 6879
www.kelloggcollection.com

Lars Bolander
212 924 1000
561 832 2121
www.larsbolander.com

Lee Jofa
800 453 3563
www.leejofa.com

Lennox Cato
+44 017 3286 5988
www.lennoxcato.com

Ligne Roset
212 253 5629
www.lignerosetny.com

Ma Maison
+44 020 7352 1181

Mark Maynard Antiques
+44 018 9261 7000
www.markmaynard.co.uk

McGuire
212 689 1565
www.kohlerinteriors.com

Mecox Gardens
800 487 4854
www.mecoxgardens.com

Mitchell Gold & Bob Williams
212 431 2575
www.mgandbw.com

Napa Valley Vintage Home
707 963 7423
www.napavalleyvintagehome.com

Newel
212 758 1970
www.newel.com

Nobilis
+44 020 8767 0774
www.nobilis.fr

Paysage
216 397 8700
www.paysage.com

Pottery Barn
888 779 5176
www.potterybarn.com

Rejuvenation
888 401 1900
www.rejuvenation.com

Robert Allen
800 333 3777
www.robertallendesign.com

Robert Young Antiques
+44 020 7228 7847
www.robertyoungantiques.com

Roche Bobois
212 889 0700
www.roche-bobois.com

Rogers de Rin
+44 020 7352 9007
www.rogersderin.co.uk

Roger's Gardens
800 647 2356
www.rogersgardens.com

Schumacher
800 523 1200
www.fschumacher.com

Smallbone of Devizes
800 763 0096
www.smallbone.co.uk

Tobias and the Angel
+44 020 8878 8902
www.tobiasandtheangel.com

Traditions Pamela Kline
518 851 3975
www.traditionspamelakline.com

Treillage Ltd.
212 988 8800
www.treillageonline.com

Wakelin & Linfield
+44 014 0370 0004
www.wakelin-linfield.com

William-Wayne & Co.
800 318 3435
www.william-wayne.com

Williams-Sonoma Home
888 922 4108
www.wshome.com

Witney Antiques
+44 019 9370 3902
www.witneyantiques.com

Woodson & Rummerfield's House of
Design, Inc.
888 963 5878
www.wandrhome.com

Yves Delorme
212 439 5701
www.yvesdelorme.com

Shops

Cabbages & Roses
3 Langton Street
London SW10 0JL
United Kingdom
+44 020 7352 7333
www.cabbagesandroses.com

The Dining Room Shop
62-64 White Hart Lane
London SW13 0PZ
United Kingdom
+44 020 8878 1020
www.thediningroomshop.co.uk

Dover House Antiques & Mercantile
2000 Frankfort Avenue
Louisville, KY 40206
502 899 1699

Island Home
313 Marine Avenue
Newport Beach, CA 92662
949 673 1133

Jane Churchill
151 Sloane Street
London SW1X 9BX
United Kingdom
+44 020 7244 7427
www.janechurchill.com

Jennings & Rohn Antiques
289 Main Street South
Woodbury, CT 06798
203 263 3775
www.jenningsandrohnantiques.com

Ladew Topiary Gardens Gift Shop
3535 Jarrettsville Pike
Monkton, MD 21111
410 557 9466
www.ladewgardens.com

Linum France
Zone d'aménagement concerté Le Tourail
84660 Coustellet
France
+33 49 076 3400
www.linum-france.com

Nordic Style
109 Lots Road
London SW10 0RN
United Kingdom
+44 020 7351 1755
www.nordicstyle.com

Robert Young Antiques
68 Battersea Bridge Rd
London SW11 3AG
United Kingdom
+44 020 7228 7847
www.robertyoungantiques.com

Small Joys
11 Court Road
Bedford, NY 10506
914 234 9738

Sweet Charity Gifts
1206 West 38th Street
Austin, TX 78705
512 324 3399
www.sweetcharitygifts.org

Traditions Pamela Kline
29 Route 9H
PO Box 416
Claverack, NY 12513
518 851 3975
www.traditionspamelakline.com

White Sense
Holländergatan 27
113 59 Stockholm
Sweden
+46 70 717 5700

William Yeoward
270 Kings Road
London SW3 5AW
United Kingdom
+44 020 7349 7828
www.williamyeoward.com

**Auction Houses
(Furniture and Ceramics)**

Christie's
212 492 5485
www.christies.com

David Rago Auctions
609 397 9374
www.ragoarts.com

Dreweatt Neate
Donnington Priory Salerooms
+44 016 3555 3553
www.dnfa.com

Freemans
215 563 9275
www.freemansauction.com

James D. Julia, Inc.
207 453 7125
www.juliaauctions.com

Lots Road Auctions
+44 020 7376 6899
www.lotsroad.com

Lyon and Turnbull
+44 013 1557 8844
www.lyonandturnbull.com

Madison
214 528 8118
www.kkmadison.com

Northeast Auctions
603 433 8400
www.northeastauctions.com

Pook & Pook
610 269 4040
www.pookandpook.com

Quittenbaum
+49 89 2737 02125
www.quittenbaum.de

Skinner, Inc.
617 350 5400
www.skinnerinc.com

Sotheby's
212 606 7000
www.sothebys.com

Stair Galleries
518 751 1000
www.stairgalleries.com

Tennants
+44 019 6962 3780
www.tennants.co.uk

von Zezschwitz
+49 89 38 98 930
www.von-zezschwitz.de

Woolley & Wallis
+44 017 2242 4500
www.woolleyandwallis.co.uk

Architectural Salvage

Adkins Architectural Antiques &
Treasures
800 522 6547
www.adkinsantiques.com

Antique Architecture
619 583 3791
www.ancientarchitecture.com

Architectural Antiquities
207 326 4938
www.archantiquities.com

Architectural Emporium
724 746 4301
www.architectural-emporium.com

The Architectural Reclaim Center
+44 020 8809 7509
www.architecturalreclaim.com

Architectural Salvage, W.D. Inc.
502 589 0670
www.architecturalsalvage.com

Architectural Salvage of San Diego
619 696 1313
www.architecturalsalvagesd.com

Architiques
607 432 9890
www.architiques.net

Aurora Mills Architectural Salvage
503 678 6083
www.auroramills.com
Carlos Castañeda Antique Hardware
and Locksmith
323 954 1717
www.carloscastanedaantiques.com

Côté Jardin Antiques
800 505 3067
www.cotejardinantiques.com

Decorations of Palm Beach
561 655 9727
www.decorationspb.com

Lassco
+44 020 7394 2100
www.lassco.co.uk

Liz's Antique Hardware
323 939 4403
www.lahardware.com

Objects in the Loft
561 659 0403
www.objectsintheloft.com

Olde Good Things
888 233 9678
www.oldegoodthings.com

The Old House Parts Company
888 743 1353
www.oldhouseparts.com

Pinch of the Past Architectural Antiques
912 232 5563
912 656 4290
www.pinchofthepast.net

ReStore
215 634 3474
www.re-store-online.com

Salvage One
312 733 0098
www.salvageone.com

Sarasota Architectural Salvage
941 362 0803
www.sarasotasalvage.com

Valerie M. Interiors
561 671 9959
www.valerieminteriors.com

Walcot Reclamation
+44 012 2544 4404
www.walcot.com

Word of Mouth
561 471 5300
www.wom-antiques.com

author's acknowledgments

Coming from the beautiful Scottish countryside and now living mainly in the city, this book has taken me back to my roots. From the high desert of Santa Fe to the wild expanses of the Adirondacks, from the icy tones of Scandinavia to the color assault that is Marrakesh, all the locations we have visited have been inspirational. I want to say an enormous thanks to all the owners who allowed us to share their homes. I would like to thank my friend and publisher Jacqui Small for all our work and travels together. Simon Upton is quite simply the best interiors photographer—he perfectly captures the mood of the homes. Thanks to Lesley Felce who has managed to keep calm and good humored. Thanks to my excellent editor Sian Parkhouse and to the inspired designer Maggie Town—this book's journey has been an interesting experience. Jill Bace has been inspirational contributing to the text. Nadine Bazar helped find some wonderful locations, as did my dear friend Gloria Stewart.

photo credits

Every effort has been made to trace the copyright holders, architects, and designers and we apologize in advance for any unintentional omissions and would be pleased to insert the appropriate acknowledgement in any subsequent edition.

1 Casa Lavacchio, Tuscany designed by Piero Castellini Baldissera; 2–3 Ebba Lopez's house in the South of France; 3 a house in Litchfield, Connecticut, designed by Champalimaud Design; 4 La Scuola, Mimmi O'Connell's house in Tuscany; 6–7 Casa Fontanella, Tuscany designed by Piero Castellini Baldissera; 8 Brad & Leslie Burnside's house in New Mexico, designed by Archaeo Architects; 9 Casa Fontanella, Tuscany designed by Piero Castellini Baldissera; 10 left a farmhouse near Toulouse designed by Kathryn Ireland; 10 center Casa Fontanella, Tuscany designed by Piero Castellini Baldissera; 10 right a house in Santa Fe, designed by Baker-Laporte & Associates; 11 center Mr & Mrs Sagbakken's cabin by the sea (Norway), interior design by Helene Forbes-Hennie; 12 Peter and Marijke de Wit of Domaine d'Heerstaayen in the Netherlands; 13 Julie Prisca's house in Normandy; 14 left Greg Wetzel and Steve Cameron's house in Santa Fe, designed by Archaeo Architects; 15 Anthony Collett's house in Tuscany; 16 Kitchen designed by Johnny Grey; 17 above Patrick Clifford's house in Auckland designed by Architectus; 17 below Wingate Jackson, Jr and Paul Trantanella's house in upstate New York; 18 Greg Wetzel and Steve Cameron's house in Santa Fe, designed by Archaeo Architects; 19 Eric & Gloria Stewart's manor house in the South West France; 20 John Saladino's home in California; 21 above a house in New Mexico, designed by Champalimaud Design; 21 center Mr & Mrs Sagbakken's cabin by the sea (Norway), interior design by Helene Forbes-Hennie; 21 below Mr & Mrs Stokke's cabin in the Norwegian mountains, interior design by Helene Forbes-Hennie; 22 above a house designed by Ilaria Miani; 22 below Brad & Leslie Burnside's house in New Mexico, designed by Archaeo Architects; 23 Mr & Mrs Stokke's cabin in the Norwegian mountains, interior design by Helene Forbes-Hennie; 24 left La Scuola , Mimmi O'Connell's house in Tuscany; 24 right a house in Santa Fe, designed by Baker-Laporte & Associates; 26 a house in Connecticut designed by Jeffrey Bilhuber; 27 James Gager & Richard Ferretti's Pennsylvanian house; 28-29 a house in Santa Fe, designed by Baker-Laporte & Associates ; 30 a house in Italy designed by Paolo Badesco; 31 above Axel Vervoordt's house in Belgium; 31 below Casa Fontanella, Tuscany designed by Piero Castellini Baldissera; 32 above a house in Oxfordshire designed by Todhunter Earle; 32 below from Mary Mullane's house in Claverack, New York; 33 Eric & Gloria Stewart's manor house in the South West France; 34 Anthony Collett's house in Tuscany; 35 Casa Lavacchio, Tuscany designed by Piero Castellini Baldissera; 36 Silvio Rech & Lesley Carstens' house near Johannesburg; 37 above a house in Marrakesh, designed by Karl Fournier and Olivier Marty, Studio KO; 37 below Silvio Rech & Lesley Carstens' house near Johannesburg; 38 Casa Fontanella, Tuscany designed by Piero Castellini Baldissera; 39 a house in Tuscany, designed by Isabelle de Borchgrave; 40 above Eric & Gloria Stewart's manor house in the South West France; 40 below Axel Vervoordt's house in Belgium; 41 Ilaria Miani's guest house; 42–43 Eric & Gloria Stewart's manor house in the South West France; 44 above a house in Tuscany, designed by Isabelle de Borchgrave; 44 below Robert & Josyane Young's house in London; 45 Robert & Josyane Young's house in London; 46 a house in Tuscany, designed by Isabelle de Borchgrave; 47 above Casa Fontanella, Tuscany designed by Piero Castellini Baldissera; 47 below a house in Tuscany, designed by Isabelle de Borchgrave; 48–49 Casa Lavacchio, Tuscany designed by Piero Castellini Baldissera; 51 top Tricia Foley's home on Long Island, tableware by Wedgwood; 51 above a house in Connecticut designed by Jeffrey Bilhuber; 51 center left Axel Vervoordt's house in Belgium; 51 center right and below left La Scuola, Mimmi O'Connell's house in Tuscany; 51 below right Dynamo camp, designed by Ilaria Miani; 52 La Scuola, Mimmi O'Connell's house in Tuscany; 53 Dynamo camp, designed by Ilaria Miani; 54 Tricia Foley's home on Long Island, tableware by Wedgwood; 55 above La Scuola, Mimmi O'Connell's house in Tuscany; 55 below Barbara Pershyn-Davis' house in upstate New York; 56 above and center Michael Leva's house in Connecticut; 56 below Mr & Mrs Stokke's cabin in the Norwegian mountains, interior design by Helene Forbes-Hennie; 57 Nicolette Schouten designer, Collection Privée; 58 above Martine Colliander of White Sense's apartment in Stockholm, Sweden; 58 below Anna Bonde's house in Provence; 59 a house in Tuscany, designed by Isabelle de Borchgrave; 60 right Architect Gilles Pellerin's house in Cannes; 61 Architect Gilles Pellerin's house in Cannes; 62 Peter and Marijke de Wit of Domaine d'Heerstaayen in the Netherlands; 63 left Mary Mullane's house in Claverack, New York; 63 right Mr & Mrs Sagbakken's cabin by the sea (Norway), interior design by Helene Forbes-Hennie; 64 left The Hotelito in Mexico, designed by Jenny Armit; 64 right Moussie Sayers of Nordic Style's house in London; 65 a home featuring Jane Churchill fabrics; 66 Dominique Kieffer's house in Normandy; 67 above left Dominique Kieffer's house in Normandy; 67 above right a house in Litchfield, Connecticut, designed by Champalimaud Design; 67 below Dominique Kieffer's house in Normandy; 68 Casa Fontanella, Tuscany designed by Piero Castellini Baldissera; 69 Casa Fontanella, Tuscany designed by Piero Castellini Baldissera; 70 A house in Watermill, Long Island, designed by Naomi Leff & Associates; 71 Pamela Kline (of Traditions)'s home in Claverack, New York; 72 Dynamo camp, designed by Ilaria Miani; 73 Julie Prisca's house in Normandy; 74 a house in Litchfield, Connecticut, designed by Champalimaud Design; 75 above left Jackye Lanham's home in Atlanta; 75 above right Warner Johnson's house in Claverack, New York; 75 below Dynamo camp, designed by Ilaria Miani; 76 left a house in Litchfield, Connecticut, designed by Champalimaud Design; 76 right Bed of Flowers, in The Netherlands, designed by Floriene Bosch; 77 Graham Head (of ABC Carpet & Home) and Barbara Rathborne's house in Long Island; 78 above Anthony Collett's house in Tuscany; 78 below left a house in Litchfield, Connecticut, designed by Champalimaud Design; 78 below right Axel Vervoodt's house in Belgium; 79 designer Lena Proudlock; 80 Eric & Gloria Stewart's manor house in the South West France; 81 above left Eric & Gloria Stewart's manor house in the South West France; 81 below left and right Marianne von Kantzow of Solgården's house in Stockholm; 82 left Anthony Collett's house in Tuscany; 82 right Mrs Fasting's cabin in the Norwegian mountains, interior design by Heiberg Cummings Design; 83 Ebba Lopez's house in the South of France; 84 Dominique Kieffer's house in Normandy; 85 above a house in Connecticut designed by Jeffrey Bilhuber; 85 center Barbara Pershyn-Davis' house in upstate New York; 85 below a house in Litchfield, Connecticut, designed by Champalimaud Design; 86 left Dominique Kieffer's house in Normandy; 86 right Bed of Flowers, in The Netherlands, designed by Floriene Bosch; 87 Dominique Kieffer's house in Normandy; 89 top a house in Tuscany, designed by Isabelle de Borchgrave; 89 above left and right a house in Litchfield, Connecticut, designed by Champalimaud Design; 89 center Casa Fontanella, Tuscany designed by Piero Castellini Baldissera; 89 below right Faulkner's house in upstate New York; 90 Dynamo camp, designed by Ilaria Miani; 91 Eric & Gloria Stewart's manor house in the South West France; 92 houses in Santa Fe, designed by Baker-Laporte & Associates; 93 a house in Virginia designed by Solis Betancourt; 94–95 Ilaria Miani's guest house; 96 Casa Fontanella, Tuscany designed by Piero Castellini Baldissera; 97 above Warner Johnson's house in Claverack, New York; 97 center Casa Fontanella, Tuscany designed by Piero Castellini Baldissera; 97 below Faulkner's house in upstate New York; 98 below Casa Fontanella, Tuscany designed by Piero Castellini; 100-101 a house in Litchfield, Connecticut, designed by Champalimaud Design; 102 Ilaria Miani's guest house; 103 above Dominique Kieffer's house in Normandy; 103 below Monteverdi Residence Club, designed by Ilaria Miani; 104 Monteverdi Residence Club, designed by Ilaria Miani; 105 a house in Tuscany, designed by Isabelle de Borchgrave; 106-107 Anthony Collett's house in Tuscany; 108 left Riyad Edward in Marrakesh designed by Stephen Skinner; 108 center Agnès Emery's house in Marrakesh; 108 right a home featuring Jane Churchill fabrics; 109 a farmhouse near Toulouse designed by Kathryn Ireland; 110 a house in Litchfield, Connecticut, designed by Champalimaud Design; 111 above a house in Litchfield, Connecticut, designed by Champalimaud Design; 111 below a house in Delhi, designed by Abraham & Thakore; 113 top Bed of Flowers, in The Netherlands, designed by Floriene Bosch; 113 above left Javier Sordo Madaleno, Architect, Mexico City; 113 above right and center The Hotelito, Mexico, designed by Jenny Armit; 113 center The Hotelito, Mexico, designed by Jenny Armit; 113 below left The Interior Archive/an apartment in Jaipur designed by Liza Bruce and Nicholas Alvis Vega; 113 below right a house in Delhi, designed by Abraham & Thakore; 114–119 Bed of Flowers, in the Netherlands, designed by Floriene Bosch; 120–21 The Interior Archive/an apartment in Jaipur designed by Liza Bruce and Nicholas Alvis Vega; 122–23 Dar Tamsna, La Palmeraie, Marrakesh; 124 Karim El Achak's house in Marrakesh; 125 above Dar Tamsna, La Palmeraie, Marrakesh; 125 below Las Alamandas, Jalisco, Mexico; 126 Las Alamandas, Jalisco, Mexico;127 above Las Alamandas, Jalisco, Mexico; 127 below The Hotelito, Mexico, designed by Jenny Armit; 128 Karim El Achak's house in Marrakesh; 129 The Hotelito, Mexico, designed by Jenny Armit; 130 Bed of Flowers, in The Netherlands, designed by Floriene Bosch; 133 top Bed of Flowers, The Netherlands, designed by Floriene Bosch; 133 above left Wingate Jackson, Jr and Paul Trantanella's house in upstate New York; 133 above right a house in Litchfield, Connecticut, designed by Champalimaud Design; 133 center William Yeoward's house in the country ; 133 below left Monteverdi Residence Club, designed by Ilaria Miani; 133 below right a house in Litchfield, Connecticut, designed by Champalimaud Design; 134 Ilaria Miani's guest house; 135 Anthony Collet's house in Tuscany; 135 Anthony Collett's house in Tuscany; 136 Marianne von Kantzow of Solgården's house in Stockholm; 137 left Marianne von Kantzow of Solgården's house in Stockholm; 137 right Bed of Flowers, in The Netherlands, designed by Floriene Bosch; 138 above Stephane and Victoria du Roure's home in New Hampshire; 138 below Warner Johnson's house in Claverack, New York; 139 La Scuola, Mimmi O'Connell's house in Tuscany; 140 Anthony Collett's house in Tuscany; 141 left a house in Litchfield, Connecticut, designed by Champalimaud Design; 141 right Pamela Kline (of Traditions)'s home in Claverack, New York; 142 left Monteverdi Residence Club, designed by Ilaria Miani; 142 center Pamela Kline (of Traditions)'s Home in Claverack, New York; 142 right Ilaria Miani's guest house; 143 a house in Tuscany, designed by Isabelle de Borchgrave; 144 Christina Strutt of Cabbages & Roses' house in Gloucestershire; 145 above left a house in Litchfield, Connecticut, designed by Champalimaud Design; 145 above right Eric & Gloria Stewart's manor house in the South West France; 145 below left Marianne von Kantzow of Solgården's house in Stockholm; 145 below right Robert & Josyane Young's house in London; 146-147 La Scuola, Mimmi O'Connell's house in Tuscany; 148 left La Scuola, Mimmi O'Connell's house in Tuscany; 148 right Casa Fontanella, Tuscany designed by Piero Castellini Baldissera; 149 Ilaria Miani's guest house; 150 above left Pamela Kline (of Traditions)'s home in Claverack, New York; 150 above right La Scuola, Mimmi O'Connoll's house in Tuscany; 150 below left La Scuola, Mimmi O'Connell's house in Tuscany; 150 below right Ilaria Miani's guest house; 151 Barbara Pershyn-Davis' house in upstate New York; 152 above a house in Provence designed by Jean-Louis Raynaud & Kenyon Kramer; 152 below Laurence Ambrose's house in Provence; 153 Casa Fontanella, Tuscany designed by Piero Castellini Baldissera; 154 above left and below right Ilaria Miani; 154 above right Fritz & Dana Rohn; 156 a house in Virginia designed by Solis Betancourt; 157 above and below Ann Mollo's house in London; 157 center a home featuring Jane Churchill fabrics; 158 above Moussie Sayers of Nordic Style's house in London; 158 below Caroline Clifton-Mogg's house in London; 159 Kate Dyson of The Dining Room Shop's house in London; 160 Stephanie Reeve's home in Atlanta, Georgia; 161 Dining room designed by Stephanie Stokes Inc, Interior Design; 162–63 Bed of Flowers, in The Netherlands, designed by Floriene Bosch; 164 a house in Provence designed by Jean-Louis Raynaud & Kenyon Kramer; 165 a farmhouse near Toulouse designed by Kathryn Ireland; 171 Anthony Collett's house in Tuscany